The Prestige Seri

Caerphilly

Michael Yelton

ISBN 9781905304509

Printed and bound in Great Britain by 4edge Ltd, Hockley, Essex.

CONTENTS

Title page: In 1968 No. 13 (13 SNY), one of the 36ft Massey-bodied Leopards of 1961, was still double-manned as it leaves the Caerphilly terminus, with the conductor jauntily observing the town.

Below: Number 11 (GTX 311), the second Saunders-bodied Foden shown after repainting with more cream, in Station Terrace, Caerphilly.

INTRODUCTION

The Caerphilly UDC undertaking was substantially larger than its neighbours run by the Councils of Gelligaer and of Bedwas & Machen, and had more interurban running from an earlier date. In fact, the local authority was so successful in its bid to run services from the town that after the Road Traffic Act 1930 there was only one route into Caerphilly run by Western Welsh (the Newport-Caerphilly-Ystrad Mynach-Bargoed service) and none run by Red & White.

The town of Caerphilly is well known not only for the eponymous cheese but also because of its very substantial ruined and partly restored castle, which dominates the centre of the urban area. It is the second largest castle in the United Kingdom after Windsor and the leaning tower featured on the UDC crest, which was introduced in 1931.

Although the Caerphilly area had a number of substantial pits, of which the best known was that at Senghenydd, which was the scene of the worst ever underground disaster in Wales, when 400 miners were killed there in 1913, the town itself was far less dependent on coal than were many adjoining places. The Urban District, which was established under the Local Government Act 1894, covered a considerable area around, including not only Senghenydd but also the village of Nelson, north-west of Caerphilly and near to the commencement of the valley leading up to Merthyr, and also part of the important commercial centre of Ystrad Mynach, which was in fact more closely connected with areas within the adjoining Gelligaer Urban District and was served largely by buses of that undertaking.

Caerphilly itself developed, particularly after the Second World War, as a dormitory town, especially for Cardiff, and also exploited its position as a crossroads where routes across from Pontypridd to Newport met those running north from Cardiff to the Valleys. It also had for many years a substantial works of the Great Western Railway, later taken over by British Rail.

Although the direct road between Cardiff and Caerphilly was little built up and also had some extremely steep gradients, which resulted in it being little used by public transport until recently, there was an alternative but longer route which was much easier and was thereby adopted as the principal way for buses to reach the capital. However, much of the commuting from Caerphilly was done by train: the line tunnelled under the mountain and was therefore direct and speedy. From the very beginning of local bus operation in Caerphilly, the vicinity of the railway station was used as the terminus, so as to facilitate interchange and this has been developed to the present travel centre.

The population of the Caerphilly Urban District increased steadily but not spectacularly over the period when it ran its own undertaking. It was about 30,000 in 1911 and about 40,000 in 1971: this again, although not atypical over large parts of the United Kingdom, contrasted greatly with towns such as Aberdare and Merthyr which lost large numbers of inhabitants over that period. In Caerphilly too it was the town itself which increased greatly in numbers and many of the outlying areas lost people. The size of the Urban District was about 15,000 acres.

Caerphilly was one of a number of local municipalities with a transport undertaking: it bordered Merthyr, Pontypridd, Gelligaer and Bedwas & Machen, and also Bedwellty and Mynyddislwyn, which together set up the West Monmouthshire Omnibus Board. In fact, the only local authority in the immediate area which did not run its own buses was Mountain Ash UDC, which remained served by private enterprise, although even there an early and unsuccessful application for tramway powers had been made.

Caerphilly was also similar to its immediate neighbours Gelligaer and Bedwas & Machen in starting running buses in areas where there had been no trams or trolleybuses and where in any event the capital equipment required for such operations would have been far too expensive for the traffic which was generated.

Caerphilly had a large number of low bridges in and around. This meant that until 1967 the undertaking never operated conventional front-engined double deckers built to anything other than the unpopular lowbridge layout, and in one particular case, the direct route to Senghenydd via Mill Road, only single deckers could be used. The last was an important restriction, because the Senghenydd route was well used and as a result there was pressure on the Council to obtain large-capacity single deckers when they became available. In later years many of the railway bridges were demolished, particular that at Maes-y-cwmmer on the Cardiff-Caerphilly-Blackwood-Tredegar service run jointly by Caerphilly and Cardiff Corporations and the West Monmouthshire Omnibus Board, but by that time the need for double-deck operation was in any event diminishing.

Under the Local Government Act 1972, which took effect on 1st April 1974, the Urban District of Caerphilly ceased to exist. It was also transferred from the historic county of Glamorganshire to the new county of Mid-Glamorgan, and incorporated into the new Rhymney Valley District Council, which also included most of the former Gelligaer Urban District and also Bedwas & Machen and Rhymney Urban Districts and part of Bedwellty. The effect on the transport undertaking is set out later. Since that time, the urban area of Caerphilly itself has developed very considerably, with large new housing estates all around what had been a small town, and many of the incomers commuting to Cardiff.

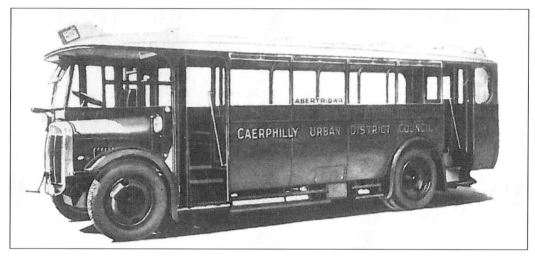

Above: Number 12 (TX 5779) arrived in 1928 and was a Tilling-Stevens Express with dual entrance bodywork by W Lewis of Cardiff.

Dennis Lancet II with Dennis bodywork, No. 31 (CTX 947), shown in Caerphilly in July 1949, after the bodywork had been rebuilt locally by Welsh Metal Industries.

HISTORY OF THE UNDERTAKING 1920-45

It is somewhat ironic, bearing in mind the later history of public transport in the area, that the first bus routes to and from Caerphilly were run by private enterprise. The South Wales Transport Company Ltd, which was based much further west in Swansea, began a service from Caerphilly to Bargoed via Ystrad Mynach in July 1915 and a further service from Caerphilly to Senghenydd in May 1916. However, these services ceased operating in May 1917, both because of the difficulties with supplies and spares resulting from the First World War and, more particularly, because the Council made it apparent that it wished to operate its own services.

On 2nd August 1917 Acts of Parliament granting powers to operate buses to both Caerphilly, which was in Glamorgan, and the neighbouring Bedwas & Machen UDC, in Monmouthshire, were passed. It was clearly envisaged that the two Councils would cooperate closely together and would set up a joint committee, for which specific powers were given in each Act, or at the very least enter into running arrangements, for which such powers were also given. The actual operating powers given to Caerphilly by the Act were very restricted. Running powers were only (a) Caerphilly to Penyrheol and Senghenydd, (b) Caerphilly to Bedwas Bridge, (c) Bedwas Bridge to Trethomas, provided Bedwas & Machen agreed, and (d) anywhere else within its own district if authorised by a provisional order under the statute. Paragraphs (b) and (c) were specifically to cater for the proposed joint route with Bedwas & Machen.

In fact, Caerphilly began using the powers given to it far earlier than did Bedwas, the first operations of which were not until January 1922. Nothing, however, was done immediately after the powers had been granted, and it was then resolved to take no action in any event until the War had ended.

Immediately after the cessation of hostilities in November 1918 the Council decided to move forward and they ordered vehicles from Tilling-Stevens in Maidstone. However, there was a considerable delay in dealing with the order and as late as February 1920 they had still not arrived:

they were then promised for the end of March. In the meantime, the Council had taken steps to acquire land and premises in Mill Road, to the north of the town, which had been owned by Rhymney Laundry Ltd. It cost £2,050 to buy the land, and then almost £3,000 to have the buildings on it converted to make them suitable for use as a garage: these were considerable sums by the standards of the time. The Mill Road depot which was established remained in use throughout the life of the undertaking, and had a large gasholder behind it which features in many photographs of the vehicles taken at that point over the years. It has since been demolished and the entire site has been redeveloped.

The first Tillings finally arrived in April 1920. A demonstration was arranged for 20th April with a view to services then starting. Tantalisingly, the only year for which the minutes of the Council and its committees is missing in the Glamorgan Archives is 1920/1, so the exact details of the commencement are now unclear.

The first routes were from the Station to Llanbradach (Plasturtwyn Terrace), on the main road north out of town, and, possibly slightly later, past the garage and up the Aber Valley to Senghenydd, which was always the most lucrative route, despite being in competition with a branch line.

The early vehicles of the undertaking were mostly supplied by Tilling-Stevens, but some of the details are not now clear and the life of buses at that time was quite short, particularly in South Wales where there were constant problems with poor roads, accentuated by steep hills and subsidence. Unlike many other municipal operators, Caerphilly was also prepared to purchase second-hand vehicles: economy drove many of the decisions which were taken, whereas in other places municipal pride precluded such buys.

Services began with two new Tilling-Stevens TS3 petrol-electric single-deckers, and later that year a further two such chassis arrived, which had been used by the War Department when carrying lorry bodies and were then rebodied. Three more Tilling-Stevens were purchased the next year, as expansion began to take place. It was noted in the Omnibus Committee on 28th June 1921 that the new buses were 'not quite in accordance with specification'.

On 8th November 1921 it was agreed that some of the Llanbradach buses should be diverted at Piccadilly Square, at the northern end of the town centre, and run up Nantgarw Road to Trecenydd, but, as with many resolutions of the Committee, this was never put into effect and the proposal was suspended, never to be revived in that form. What did happen was the approval for the extension of the Llanbradach service to Ystrad Mynach (Royal Oak), initially as an experiment for one month, as the road had been improved. The settlement of Ystrad Mynach was mostly in Caerphilly but partly in Gelligaer and in May 1922 the latter authority (which at that time was not running its own services) agreed to the former running to the Beech Hotel in the centre of the town. Local sensibilities were often much more important than the convenience of the travelling public, but on this occasion the fare paying passengers were benefited.

There were, however, serious difficulties between Caerphilly and its near, but much smaller, neighbour Bedwas & Machen, in the early years. As early as September 1919 the latter proposed running four times a day to Machen but much more frequently to Trethomas, which lay between the two villages in its title and was at the limit of Caerphilly's powers. However, the proposal then went to sleep for some time, and it was not until March 1921 that Caerphilly agreed in general terms to Bedwas' request to run into their area and indeed on 22nd September 1921 approved the draft timetable. It was not until 6th January 1922 that representatives of the two councils met formally to discuss timetables and the like. Caerphilly wanted to run alternate weeks, which was clearly unacceptable to Bedwas as it meant that the latter's vehicles would be unused for half the year. It was eventually agreed, on 11th January 1922, that in alternate weeks one of the two Councils would run until mid-afternoon, and thereafter there should be joint operation: the traditional form of timetable for South Wales was used whereby the frequency increased as the day went on. This was in order to allow Bedwas, which by then had purchased vehicles, to operate them with effect from the next day.

In March 1922 there was further wrangling, leading to a suggestion by Caerphilly that they would run only so far as Bedwas Bridge. On 17th March 1922 Caerphilly told Bedwas that they would have to withdraw from their area, to which Bedwas replied that Caerphilly could not renage from the consent they had given to allow them to cross the boundary. On 20th June 1922 there was a meeting at which Caerphilly finally conceded the principle of joint running throughout, which Bedwas had always wanted, but by then there was so much mistrust between the two that Bedwas refused the offer which they had always asked for. Caerphilly then decided to take legal advice.

Matters finally came to a head in early 1923 when Caerphilly went so far as to bring an action in the High Court asking for an injunction to prevent Bedwas running in their area. Although the plaintiffs took a very hard line initially against their smaller neighbour, the action was settled on 23rd March 1923 on terms that Bedwas ran the service from Caerphilly to Trethomas until 3 pm, then both councils operated jointly thereafter, with extra buses on Friday and Saturdays. The consequence of this was that a joint committee of the two councils was finally instituted, which first met on 18th May 1923, at which the agreement on which the action had been settled was again accepted and was thereafter acted upon. Caerphilly then took objection to Bedwas running to Machen, which they themselves could not do, and it was not until 13th June 1924 that peace finally reigned, and the agreement made on a temporary basis in 1923 was made permanent. However, there remained suspicion between the two neighbours and other local municipalities, accentuated by a number of proposals, the first in 1927, to create a transport board for the whole Rhymney Valley, which Bedwas saw as an end to its independence and West Mon resented in principle.

In the meantime, the omnibus department began to take shape. On 7th February 1922 it was decided to employ a full time manager, but, in a characteristic episode of small town politics, the decision was reconsidered and deferred on 4th April 1922. Finally, the original inspector, ET O'Connor, was made temporary manager, and then in July 1923 his position was made permanent. This made the running of the organisation much easier and in November 1923 bye-laws came into force to govern the terms of travel. Earlier, in November 1922, the councillors had taken offence at being questioned by one of the conductors as to whether they were undergoing official business whenever they claimed not to have to pay.

One problem common to all the small municipal operators in South Wales continued: the councillors micromanaged the undertaking and the manager had to refer every minor problem to the Omnibus Committee, including appeals against his own disciplinary actions. A great deal of time was wasted on trivia, and perhaps less attention than was appropriate paid to the wider picture. Decisions costing a great deal of money were given no more prominence than issues involving a discrepancy on the waybill of a few pennies.

The increasing needs of the undertaking saw an advertisement placed in May 1922 for a charabanc 'for extra capacity on busy days'. In July 1922 a second-hand Dennis arrived from a coal company in Ebbw Vale: there appear to be no pictures of it and it is not clear exactly how the body was configured. There was not a great deal of call for it, although early the next year the staff were told they could not use it for an excursion. It was decided to have it rebodied as a bus and to then use it, possibly one-manned, to extend the Ystrad Mynach service to Nelson. In July 1923 J Norman of Cardiff agreed to supply a new body to a design drawn up by the Council surveyor, at a cost of £324 5s 6d, and the Nelson extension opened on 3rd August 1923, although the bodybuilders were late with the Dennis and an unidentified vehicle was hired in to start the new service. In late 1926 land was rented in Nelson to allow vehicles to turn.

The settlement with Bedwas, and the stability that brought, led to further vehicles being purchased, all from Tilling-Stevens: a profit of £1,983 was made in the year ending March 1923, which augured well. The nature of the enterprise was shown by resolutions such as that in February 1924 that miners should not use the buses when still in their working clothes: this was of course before the introduction of pithead baths.

Further expansion was also considered. One of the problems of an undertaking such as this was that councillors tended to request a taxi service for their ward, with every conceivable road, however unsuitable, being put forward for a service. However, the further suggestion, as early as May 1924, that Trecenydd and possibly Penyrheol, a developing area, receive their own town service had more credence. As well as the regular services, there were, from almost the start, many workmen's specials, and in June 1924 running began from Llanbradach to Bedwas on such a basis, which led to predictable protests from the noisy neighbouring authority. However,

it became clear, certainly by 1926, that although traffic generally was on the increase (until very badly affected by the General Strike that year), the Bedwas service, which had caused so much trouble, was actually losing money for the Council.

The size of the fleet necessitated a further extension to the garage in 1926, at a cost of £2,650. There were complaints about the converted charabanc used on the Nelson service, which again was not doing well, and by late 1925 it was resolved to replace it with two light vehicles, which originally were to have been more Tillings. At about this time the service to Trecenydd began, initially on Friday and Saturday afternoons and evenings only. Here, as elsewhere in the Valleys, traffic built up during the later part of the day and was often very heavy in the late evenings.

On 19th October 1926 it was resolved to run to Nantgarw and Tongwynlais, both on the easier route to Cardiff, and also to run the Nelson service as a circular, returning via Pontypridd. The latter scheme was never taken further, and the Tongwynlais route was approved but deferred for road works. A firm called Tresilian Motors had at one stage shortly before this run from Caerphilly to Nantgarw, but had given up: both they and Cridlands, a well known local firm, had applied to run through to Cardiff, but they were told that the roads were unsuitable. Goughs, another local operator later absorbed by Red & White, asked to run to Pontypridd but again were rebuffed.

On 20th September 1927, however, Cardiff, which ran a small number of services outside its boundaries, enquired about the possibility of a through service to be run jointly by the two municipalities, and at meetings in October and December 1927 this was agreed in principle, subject to the completion of the road improvements.

In the meantime, the Caerphilly Council continued its expansionist tendencies by promoting a further Act of Parliament. This coincided with bills being put before the House by the four largest railway companies, to allow them to run bus services on their own account. As part of this initiative, the GWR asked on 18th October 1927 to purchase the Caerphilly undertaking. Local operators Lewis and James then indicated on 7th February 1928 that they too wished to purchase the operation.

On 6th March 1928 there was a meeting between Caerphilly and the GWR at which it was agreed in principle that there should be 50/50 joint operation between the two parties, presumably on the basis of a committee such as came to exist in parts of Yorkshire. On the basis of that concord, each party withdrew its opposition to the other's bill.

The Caerphilly UDC Act 1928 (passed on 2nd July of that year) gave the council power under Section 26 to run within their own district and also with the consent of the Minister and of the other local authorities to Cardiff and to Newport, but only by way of joint operations with the two County Boroughs concerned, and by Section 30 to enter into working arrangements with any other local authority or board - the latter being an obvious reference to the West Monmouthshire Omnibus Board. Oddly, at this point FE Goode, who was an employee of West Mon, and later had a short and unsatisfactory period as manager for the Board, was a councillor in Caerphilly and for a time chairman of the Omnibus Committee, but the clear conflict of interest was not raised overtly.

Following the works being done to the main road, the Tongwynlais service began every day except Sundays in December 1928. However, in April 1929 this was superseded by the joint service to Cardiff, which ran over the same route. Cardiff was anxious almost from the start to lengthen the service, but their proposition in November 1929 that it be extended northwards to Ystrad Mynach and perhaps southwards to Penarth fell on stony ground.

1928 also saw a substantial influx of new vehicles and the demise of many of the older buses. Caerphilly was always very keen on using demonstration vehicles, and after trialling Thornycroft and Tilling-Stevens on the services to Nelson and to Senghenydd, they continued with the latter manufacturer as their preferred supplier. Five new Tillings arrived, all with W Lewis dual entrance bodywork, and in the same year two small Vulcans were bought to be used as one-man vehicles to replace the rebodied charabanc on the Nelson run, with bodywork by the same company: there had also been a demonstration of that chassis. Lewis was a Tilling-Stevens agent in Cardiff as well as a bodybuilder.

In the meantime, the Great Western Railway (Road Transport) Act 1928 had been passed. The terms of that Act provided, by Section 3, that the Railway Company should not run in competition with any bus service run by a local authority save with the consent of that authority, but permitted

it to run from outside into or through the local authority area provided the same passenger was not picked up and set down within that area. By Section 11 the Railway Company was also given the power to make agreements with local authorities for joint running.

The GWR seem to have lost interest in a complete merger with Caerphilly and the matter was deferred several times before quietly being abandoned. However, the GWR did want to take over the route to Trethomas with a view to commencing a through route from Caerphilly to Newport: Caerphilly had never managed to come to agreement with Newport over this, which they needed under their own Act.

In due course, the Railway adopted the same policy in South Wales as had it and other train operators elsewhere, namely investing in road transport by using associated companies in which they had a shareholding. In the Valleys, this was done by the reconstruction of South Wales Commercial Motors Ltd and its metamorphosis into Western Welsh, the 'Western' representing the railway interest rather than any geographical reference.

In 1930 the new company took over the Caerphilly operation to Trethomas, but not that of Bedwas & Machen. It seems that having been unable to persuade Newport County Borough Council to agree to a through route, Caerphilly lost interest in the short section to Trethomas. Caerphilly never thereafter operated into Bedwas, despite its proximity, save on workers' services.

While cutting back on the service to the east of the town, and abandoning any attempt to reach Newport, there was expansion elsewhere. In December 1929 it was agreed to extend the Trecenydd route into the estate, an area known then and now as 'The Avenues'. This proved unsuccessful and in September 1930 it was again cut back to the previous terminus at The Crescent, but extended at the other end from the Cenotaph, opposite the castle in the centre of town, to the Station. On 17th March 1931 the service was discontinued completely as part of a reaction to the adverse economic climate of the time, which also involved the discontinuance for a time of many workmen's buses. By April of the same year it was decided to reinstate the Trecenydd service and this started in June. The decision in relation to workers' specials was only short term: the Caerphilly fleet was always larger than would

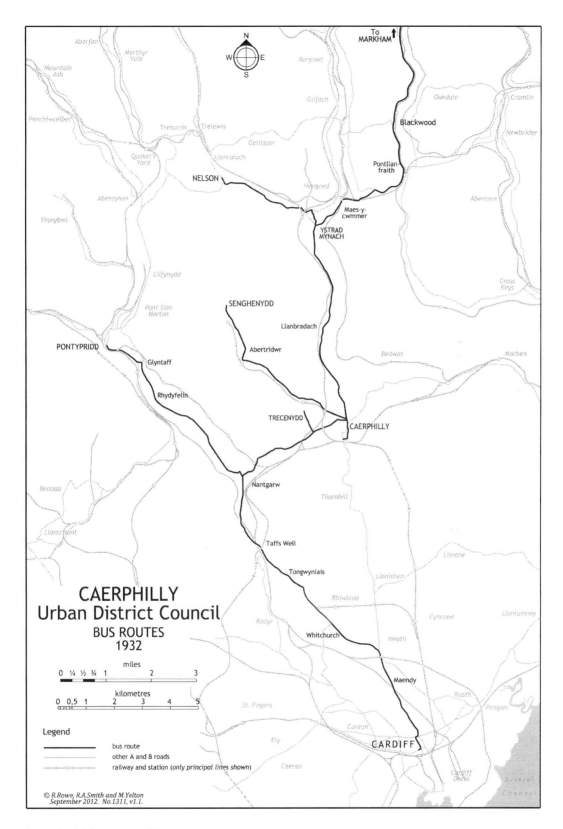

CAERPHILLY
Urban District Council
BUS ROUTES
1932

To MARKHAM

Blackwood

Pontllan-fraith

NELSON

Maes-y-cwmmer

YSTRAD MYNACH

SENGHENYDD

Llanbradach

PONTYPRIDD

Glyntaff

Abertridwr

Rhydyfelin

TRECENYDD

CAERPHILLY

Nantgarw

Taffs Well

Tongwynlais

Whitchurch

Maendy

CARDIFF

miles
| 0 | ¼ | ½ | ¾ | 1 | 2 | 3 |

kilometres
| 0 | 0,5 | 1 | 2 | 3 | 4 | 5 |

Legend
— bus route
other A and B roads
railway and station (only principal lines shown)

© R.Rowe, R.A.Smith and M.Yelton
September 2012. No.1311, v1.1.

For route details see page 67.

be thought necessary for the running of the stage services, because of the very large number of such services run, initially to the local pits (including the Navigation Colliery in Bedwas) and later to the many factories which sprung up in the area after the Second World War. There was no question at this time of the employment of double-deckers, because the only route on which they may have been justified, to Senghenydd, was barred even to lowbridge models by the Mill Road railway bridge. The Senghenydd service at that time ran to the Universal Hotel, but there was long standing pressure, which began in the 1930s, to extend to Cenydd Terrace, which was one of four rows high above the town. The road access prevented that extension ever being run during the Council's time.

The Road Traffic Act 1930 passed into law on 1st August of that year but was not to come into effect until 1st May 1931. It was apparent to all concerned that there were advantages to be gained in establishing services prior to that date. Caerphilly also took delivery of more Tilling-Stevens, this time with Eastwood and Kenning dual entrance bodies, and some second-hand Guys, which were used only for a few years.

On 29th July 1930, a few days before the passage of the Road Traffic Act, there was a conference between representatives of Caerphilly, of Cardiff and of the West Mon Board with a view to establishing new through facilities. Caerphilly already had the route north to Ystrad Mynach, and the Board ran from there to Blackwood, and also from Blackwood to Markham. The upshot was a proposal, which was agreed at the conference, to join up all these services and provide a through service from Cardiff to Markham with an equal number of buses being supplied by each of the three participants. The new service began on 10th December 1930 with initially only Caerphilly vehicles running through, but by 1931 there was full participation of all three operators. After the additional service had commenced, Caerphilly withdrew its short running to Llanbradach in March 1931.

Once the 1930 Act had been passed, the Council was in a much easier position so far as the development of new services was concerned, because it could operate anywhere within its own area and, with the consent of the Traffic Commissioners, in other areas, without requiring specific statutory powers so to do. The 1917 and 1928 Acts were therefore superseded.

Applications were made to the Commissioners, and were granted, for the following services, which formed the basis of Caerphilly's operations until the town itself began developing after the Second World War, which then required more short distance urban services:

Caerphilly-Senghenydd;
Caerphilly-Ystrad Mynach-Nelson;
Cardiff-Nantgarw-Caerphilly-Ystrad Mynach-Blackwood-Markham (jointly with Cardiff Corporation and the West Monmouthshire Omnibus Board);
Caerphilly-Trecenydd (town service), Fridays and Saturdays only.

The picture was completed when on 28th July 1931 agreement was reached with another neighbouring authority, Pontypridd UDC, for a further joint service, this time to connect the two towns. Although it had been decided to commence this in December 1931, in November Pontypridd tried to pull out, asserting they did not have appropriate vehicles: it was intended from the beginning to use one man operated single-deckers, operation of which was restricted by the 1930 Act to those with no more than 20 seats. The route began in January 1932 with Caerphilly loaning a vehicle to Pontypridd, but on 6th March 1932 both parties commenced running with their own vehicles. It always worked on approximate hourly frequency, with extras to serve the vast Trading Estate which was developed at Treforest about half way along the route, and was another interurban link in the transport of the area which was kept out of the hands of Western Welsh and Red & White. Interestingly, it is a route which under deregulation has seen the number of vehicles along it increase substantially and it now forms part of a through service from Caerphilly to the Rhondda.

The livery used initially was scarlet with cream roofs, but in 1932 this was changed completely, and from that time vehicles were painted in a distinctive and unusual but attractive dark green with black wings. There was at that time no white relief, but any beading was polished bright. The second-hand Guys were never repainted into the new livery.

In 1933 the undertaking decided to acquire two further Tilling-Stevens buses, but at this stage had decided to specify the provision of Gardner 6LW diesel engines which the Maidstone manufacturer could not supply. The order was moved to their old competitors for the Council's trade, Thornycroft, who were able to incorporate the required engines. In August 1933 two Thornycrofts with Beadle rear-entrance bodies were acquired but in the meantime Thornycroft and Beadle approached the council in July and offered to finish a further vehicle for them, to be exhibited at Olympia in November that year on the Beadle stand. Although at first the manufacturers were told that no such further bus was needed, the vehicle was in due course purchased, arriving in December 1933.

In that year Gellygaer (as it was then spelled) UDC again proposed a joint transport undertaking for the entire area, including Caerphilly and the West Mon Board, but this did not proceed. It was an idea which was floated from time to time thereafter, but never agreed. On the face of it, there was held some attraction, particularly as the economic climate was still very poor. Caerphilly was even unhappy about the new trunk service, and proposed in 1933 that it be terminated at Ystrad Mynach and in February 1934 at Blackwood. The section north to Markham was the least well patronised.

Another long running issue came to the fore at this time. The terminal facilities at Caerphilly Station were not satisfactory, because buses had to be reversed in and out owing to the lack of space. In 1934 the Railway were approached to sell an additional area. This question was to raise its head at meeting after meeting over the years.

In 1934 there was pressure from the members to run to the Miners' Hospital, which is about a mile from the Station. The initial proposal was to extend the service from Nelson, which at that time ran only every two hours, although there were also shorts from Nelson to Ystrad Mynach. Eventually more realistic counsel prevailed and it was decided to run occasionally to coincide with visiting times, which at that time were very restricted, and apart from some journeys from Nelson one trip from Senghenydd ran through on Tuesdays.

The development of the route network slowed down over the next few years. In June 1935 the lucrative Senghenydd service was extended a short distance to the Colliery Bridge. The following month consideration was given to extending the Nelson service to Cardiff via the mountainous Thornhill road, but nothing was done at that stage.

The years after 1933 saw the AEC, Thornycroft, Dennis, Bristol and Daimler concerns all supplying demonstrators: in 1936, after a considerable gap, the vote went to Dennis, who were represented locally and forcefully by DJ Davies of Merthyr, through whom orders were placed. In 1936 they supplied two Lancets with their own rear-entrance bodies and two forward control Aces also with Dennis bodies, though full-fronted and equipped for one-man-operation at that early date. They were specifically intended for the Nelson route, after the manager indicated in August 1935 that this capacity would suffice for that service, at least on Monday to Thursday and on Friday mornings. They were originally intended to have sliding doors controlled by the driver, but this was later altered to pneumatic power operation. They arrived on 1st April 1936, and after 27th May 1936 were operated as one-man vehicles between Ystrad Mynach and Nelson, and then a conductor joined for the section into Caerphilly. By so acting, one conductor could be used to assist the two drivers involved.

The vexed question of running to Cardiff via Thornhill re-emerged at this time, and after a meeting in Cardiff on 31st July 1936 it was agreed that the Nelson route would indeed run through, but only after the roads had been improved.

Another Dennis-bodied Ace followed in July 1937 although not on this occasion with a full front. It was originally intended that Davies themselves would construct the body, but eventually Dennis built it. It generally ran on the short route to Trecenydd: some councillors wanted a few journeys to be run westwards to Groes wen, but that hamlet was never served by regular services. Its other use was on the Pontypridd route. The service to the Miners' Hospital was also increased at this time for a short period so that it ran hourly.

There were problems with the engines of the Lancets which had been supplied, but Davies were obviously persuasive salesmen, and managed to convince the Council to take two more in 1938: their Dennis 04 oil engines also proved unsatisfactory and they were replaced as early as the following year. Dennis vehicles were not frequently found in the municipal sector.

In 1938 the manager left and after a temporary appointment, Clifford Thomas was appointed with effect from 17th May 1938. He was to remain in post for 25 years and see the most prosperous years of the undertaking. For all his early years, the Chairman of the Omnibus Committee was Councillor T Edwards, so there was continuity throughout.

Just before the new manager's arrival it was decided to make application for the Thornhill route. This became something of a debacle. On 1st July 1938 the Traffic Commissioners refused permission for a through route to Cardiff via the mountain road, and indicated that they would not have given permission under Section 101 of the Road Traffic Act 1930 for Caerphilly to run outside their area. Why this decision was taken is not clear, since a few journeys along that road would hardly have threatened the train service. The Council had then to apply to extend some of the Nelson services south to the Travellers Rest inn, a remote spot near the hamlet of Thornhill, and Cardiff correspondingly applied to extend a few journeys northwards from their terminus at Capel Gwilym, on the city boundary. Those applications were granted on 11th November 1938 on terms that Caerphilly did not use double-deckers, used second gear on the mountain, and did not advertise through connections to Cardiff. Such were the vagaries of the licensing system of the time. The service began on 5th February 1939, after a standing place off the twisting road had been constructed near the Travellers Rest.

There was less trouble associated with an extension of the Trecenydd route to the Bowls Inn, Penyrheol, where connections could be made for Senghenydd, from 22nd July 1938, and the establishment, finally, on that service of daily buses with effect from 27th March 1939, with many running via St. Martin's Road and the Hospital, although they still ran only in the late afternoon and evening.

The only company service into the town was run by Western Welsh. Once they had established the through service from Caerphilly to Newport via Bedwas, after taking over Caerphilly's share of the Trethomas service, they joined it to a long established but isolated Ystrad Mynach-Bargoed route by extending the latter south to Caerphilly, but giving protection to the local services over the competing section. Until 1938 they garaged one vehicle at Mill Road, but they were then told that this arrangement was no longer acceptable because of lack of available space. By the end of that year the Council was employing 29 road staff and another 12 in the garage.

The new manager established a policy of gradual renewal of the fleet combined with rebuilding of those older vehicles which remained serviceable. However, he appears not to have been impressed with the Dennis marque and to have had a penchant for Daimlers, which were not cheap but were renowned for their quality.

A Daimler COG5/40 with Willowbrook B39F body had been produced for demonstration by the bodybuilders, and was inspected in Coventry by the undertaking in December 1938, and immediately acquired. It was then the largest vehicle in the fleet, and the manager said it would be particularly useful on the new Thornhill route.

The new manager was impressed by the Daimler/Willowbrook combination and was also keen on standardisation. In April 1939 another such vehicle arrived, albeit with a then more conventional rear entrance, and shortly after the outbreak of hostilities two more were taken into the fleet, which had been ordered before the War started. The Council remained unrelentingly hostile to private enterprise running services. In 1939 IC Pursey applied to run from Caerphilly to the hamlet of Rudry, which had never been served by the UDC. They voted to oppose the application. The Rudry service was, however, always run by a local company and Caerphilly never even applied for a service there.

The outbreak of the War saw a reduction of services, and the Nelson-Ystrad Mynach shuttle ceased. Cardiff decided to retrench for the duration and left the Markham service to Caerphilly and West Mon. However, although regular services were cut back there was a need for many extra works journeys, particularly to the very large Treforest Trading Estate between Nantgarw and Pontypridd. As from 4th November 1940 the services previously run by EJ Hazell of Senghenydd, from their base to either Bedwas or Treforest, were taken over. The Senghenydd-Treforest service did not run via Caerphilly town centre, which meant that it would be possible to use double-deckers on it. The hostilities between Caerphilly and Bedwas had not, however, entirely died: even under wartime conditions, a suggestion that the Caerphilly bus carry passengers back from Bedwas instead of running dead was met with a firm refusal.

The Second World War period saw the fleet worked extremely hard, as in other places and particularly in South Wales, where operating conditions were especially difficult because of the combination of steep hills and poor roads, often the result of mining subsidence.

Initially, the Council remained faithful to single-deckers. However, new vehicles were very difficult to find, and by 1940 there was only one surviving Tilling-Stevens vehicle, which was on borrowed time. The chairman and manager were given authority to purchase a second-hand vehicle, petrol-engined if necessary. This led to the acquisition of an Albion with Plaxton coach body from HG Sage of Burry Port in West Wales, an unlikely purchase in other circumstances. This arrived in February 1941. Later that month Clifford Thomas and the chairman of the Committee went to see both Daimler and Willowbrook, perhaps not understanding that under the prevailing conditions it was impossible to buy vehicles to order as had happened pre-war. More attempts were made throughout 1941 to obtain a new vehicle, and finally Caerphilly were allocated an Albion CX13 which had originally been ordered by Red & White and was in fact one of the last Albions constructed before the Scotstoun factory went over to military production. It was intended to have a Duple centre entrance body, but this was altered before delivery to a more conventional front door. It was painted all green by the Council and began service on 26th January 1942.

Shortly after, a ten-year-old Daimler CP6 with rear entrance bus bodywork by Pickering of Wishaw, which had been new to Lanarkshire Traction, was acquired from GF Rees of Neyland, in Pembrokeshire, specifically for the Bedwas works service. A licence was granted in July 1942 for two Bedford OWBs, but these were never ordered as the Committee was doubtful about them.

The issue of using double-deckers for the first time then surfaced. The adjoining municipal operators, Gelligaer, Bedwas & Machen and West Mon had all similarly operated single-deckers only before the War and all introduced double-deckers during or shortly after it. In the summer of 1942 Pontypridd had the roadway beneath Cwrt Rawlin bridge lowered, with the consequence that double-deckers could be used on the joint service. In October 1942 Pontypridd lent Caerphilly a new Guy double-decker for training purposes.

After this the Council finally decided to take the plunge and ordered two double-deckers, primarily for services to Treforest but also with a view to using on the Cardiff-Markham service after modifications were carried out to the railway bridge at Maes-y-cwmmer. The real problem was the bridge over Mill Road, and enquiries were made about lowering the road there, but it appeared that the foundations were so shallow that this was impracticable. It was also suggested that it may be possible to run under through the middle of the carriageway, but that too proved impossible.

In 1943 a single Daimler CWA6 with Duple lowbridge body to utility standards arrived: its first day in service was 1st August. It remained the only such permanent vehicle for about six months, and in the meantime two elderly AEC Regents were borrowed from Roberts Pioneer Motor Services of Newport, Pembrokeshire.

Two more second-hand vehicles were then bought, an Albion, again with a petrol engine, with a full-fronted Plaxton coach body, originally the property of Sages of Burry Port, and later with the RAF, and a Tilling-Stevens, the first into the fleet since 1933, with a Park Royal coach body, which arrived from Bullens of Swansea. The willingness to take second-hand and at first sight unsuitable vehicles reflects the pressure the Council was under to maintain works and other vital services at this time. In early 1944 Gelligaer loaned three AEC Regals, Bedwas an OWB, and Palace Transport of Cardiff a Leyland LT1.

Although obviously the time was not ripe for service developments, there were some changes. A daily service to Thornhill (Travellers Rest) via the Miners' Hospital and the incongruously named settlement of Watford, an easier gradient than the mountain road, was proposed on 8th November 1943, but may not have started at that time, and the Markham service was diverted southwards only via Clive Street, Ludlow Street and Crescent Road into Nantgarw Road, avoiding Piccadilly Square, with effect from 14th November 1943. The manager then suggested building a completely new bus garage and station in King Edward Avenue, on the opposite side of the station from the existing terminus. New workmen's services began to Cwmbran and also to Rogerstone, which was to be a long term running sore between Caerphilly and Bedwas.

In 1944 orders for new double-deckers finally bore fruit, and the Council was allocated two

Just after the outbreak of the War, Caerphilly took delivery of two new Daimlers with rear entrance Willowbrook bodies. No. 35 (ETG 647) is shown when new, displaying its crest and the side indicator.

Daimlers with Duple bodywork and two Guy Arabs bodied by Roe. The first Daimler, FNY 515, numbered 15, began in service on 25th March 1944. It was to have a very short life indeed in the fleet and not surprisingly is not recorded on film.

On 9th April 1944, Easter Day, there was a conflagration at the depot, which occurred only a year after a similar event in Bedwas had destroyed the entire fleet. It is thought that the blaze started in the ex-RAF Albion: there were at that time 22 vehicles in service and eight of them, or more than a third of the fleet, were completely destroyed and the new Daimler double-decker was so badly damaged that it never ran again for Caerphilly and required rebodying after being sold on. The vehicles which were destroyed were No.15, the new double-decker, which was only 15 days old, No. 36, one of the Daimlers delivered just after the start of the War, No. 32, a Dennis Lancet new in 1938, No. 29, a full-fronted Dennis Ace from 1936, No. 20, the last surviving Tilling-Stevens, 8, the ex-RAF Albion, 6, the second-hand Daimler acquired in 1942, and No. 21, the second-hand Tilling-Stevens acquired in 1943, together with No. 16, the Leyland LT1 on hire from Palace Transport. It was a catastrophic blow to the undertaking.

The local municipalities rallied round, with Bedwas & Machen, Gelligaer, Pontypridd and West Mon all loaning vehicles although they themselves were very hard pressed at the time and two of the vehicles already on loan from Gelligaer were slightly damaged in the fire.

However, the three new double-deckers arrived later in 1944, and in 1945 two more Guys, one bodied by Weymann and the other by Roe. Also acquired to assist in the short term were five single-deckers, two Guys dating from 1934 and three Daimlers from 1936, all with Park Royal bus bodies and all coming from Wolverhampton Corporation. The staff immediately protested about the brakes on the Guys and said they would not drive them, so work was done on them in what remained of the garage.

The situation at the end of the War, in Caerphilly as in many other places, was that the fleet was badly worn out and such vehicles as were reasonably new were to utility standards and would require considerable rebuilding in the fairly near future. The garage needed rebuilding, but on 31st October 1944 the adjoining fire station was handed over to the omnibus department, giving extra accommodation. Double-deckers had been made part of the fleet, but still could not be used on the busiest service. That point was clearly made in early 1945 when a driver badly damaged one of the Daimler utilities by driving it under Mill Road bridge.

Roe-bodied Guy utility No, 19 (FNY 719) is seen in Caerphilly in 1954 still carrying the old application of the livery.

HISTORY OF THE UNDERTAKING 1945-74

The first significant event in the annals of the undertaking after the end of the War was the joint takeover in 1945 by it, Pontypridd UDC, Gelligaer UDC and the West Monmouthshire Omnibus Board, of the business of Jones Brothers (Treharris) Ltd, trading as Commercial Motor Service, which was a well established business with two basic routes, Pontypridd-Treharris-Nelson-Ystrad Mynach-Blackwood and Pontypridd-Nelson-Bedlinog, with additional short workings from Pontypridd to Treharris.

The undertaking had originally been offered for sale for £35,000 to Gelligaer, and then to the four eventual purchasers and to Merthyr Borough Council. Merthyr were not interested at all and the others were not interested at the original price. However, they speedily knocked the vendors down to £25,000 and acquired the business with effect from 1st November 1945, although the agreement between the four of them was not concluded until 4th February 1946. The Blackwood service ran through Maes-y-cwmmer, a far corner of Bedwas & Machen, but that Council was not involved in the negotiations or the purchase.

Caerphilly had perhaps the least to gain from the purchase, although Nelson was just within its area, as was the road from there to Ystrad Mynach. Pontypridd and the West Mon Board controlled two of the termini, and Gelligaer already ran to Bedlinog, which was then within its boundary, on an existing route from Bargoed: ironically the village is now part of Merthyr, the authority which did not wish to purchase, in which area was also situated the Jones garage at Treharris. Caerphilly and West Mon thereafter normally ran the Pontypridd-Blackwood service, Caerphilly starting at the Pontypridd end and West Mon at Blackwood. Gelligaer ran the Bedlinog service jointly with Red & White (as Jones had done) and Pontypridd ran extras and weekend runnings on both routes and on the short journeys. Caerphilly did not run on Sundays.

Caerphilly thereafter administered the pool for what were termed the ex-CMS Services: there were quarterly meetings between the four participants. Thus Caerphilly's accounts required separate figures being compiled for their own services, for the joint route to Pontypridd, for the joint route from Cardiff to Markham, and for the ex-CMS services.

The rather run down Jones Brothers fleet was divided between the acquiring undertakings. Caerphilly received an elderly Dennis which they never used, a 1938 diesel-engined Dennis Lancet with Willowbrook body which fitted in well with their existing fleet, and a solitary Bedford OWB.

After the War, vehicles acquired cream relief, although the dark green livery was retained. Single-deckers had one cream band below the windows, double-deckers three in all, and one was even delivered in reversed livery, which it wore for about two years.

There were further important developments in the immediate post-war years as the demand for travel exploded.

With effect from 21st May 1945 the Caerphilly-Nelson service was run hourly and on occasion double-deckers were used. This was a real change from the pre-war position when small one-man vehicles ran these journeys: it was even suggested that the frequency increase to half hourly, but this never happened. There was a meeting with Cardiff, who indicated that they wished in due course to return to participating on the Markham service, and to make connections at Thornhill or Capel Gwilym but without through services on that road. That latter route began operating again from Caerphilly on 5th November 1945 and some journeys ran via Watford. There was an increase in services to Trecenydd, which at this time had reverted to Fridays and Saturdays only.

Markham was not the natural terminus for the Cardiff service, but prior to 1939 Western Welsh and Red & White, who ran a frequent and very lucrative Newport-Blackwood-Markham-Tredegar service, the subject of great jealousy from West Mon as it ran right through their area, had resisted any attempted by the municipalities to extend their service to Tredegar. After the War, the Traffic Commissioners indicated that they regarded it as impossible to resist such an application. It was made on 28th January 1947, but initially deferred and it was not until 29th February 1948 that the trunk route was run right through. Its basic frequency was hourly on Sunday to Friday and half hourly on Saturdays, but on Fridays there was an additional hourly service

BLACKWOOD-----PONTYPRIDD SERVICE.

	A.m.	A.m.		P.m.	P.m.	P.m.
Pontypridd	7.20	8.20		8.20	9.20	10.20
Travellers Rest	7.35	8.35	And	8.35	9.35	10.35
Treharris	7.45	8.45		8.45	9.45	10.45
Trelewis	7.50	8.50	every	8.50	9.50	10.50
Nelson	7.55	8.55		8.55	9.55	10.55
Ystrad Mynach	8.06	9.06	Hour	9.06	10.06	11.06
Maesycwmmer	8.09	9.09		9.09	10.09	11.09
Pontllanfraith	8.12	9.12	until	9.12	10.12	11.12
Blackwood.	8.16	9.16		9.16	10.16	11.16

	A.m.	A.m.		P.m.	P.m.	P.m.
Blackwood	7.15	8.25		8.25	9.25	10.25
Pontllanfraith	7.18	8.28	And	8.28	9.28	10.28
Maesycwmmer	7.22	8.32		8.32	9.32	10.32
Ystrad Mynach	7.25	8.35	every	8.35	9.35	10.35
Nelson	7.45	8.45		8.45	9.45	10.45
Trelewis	7.50	8.50	Hour	8.50	9.50	10.50
Treharris	7.55	8.55		8.55	9.55	10.55
Travellers Rest	8.05	9.05	until	9.05	10.05	11.05
Pontypridd.	8.18	9.18		9.18	10.18	11.18

PONTYPRIDD ---- TREHARRIS SERVICE

	P.m.	P.m.	P.m.	P.m.	P.m.	P.m.	P.m.	P.m.
Pontypridd	1.05	2.05	3.05	4.05	5.05	6.05	7.05	8.05
Travellers Rest	1.15	2.15	3.15	4.15	5.15	6.15	7.15	8.15
Treharris	1.35	2.35	3.35	4.35	5.35	6.35	7.35	8.35

	P.m.	P.m.	P.m.	P.m.	P.m.	P.m.	P.m.	P.m.
Treharris	1.40	2.40	3.40	4.40	5.40	6.40	7.40	8.40
Travellers Rest	1.50	2.50	3.50	4.50	5.50	6.50	7.50	8.50
Pontypridd	2.00	3.00	4.00	5.00	6.00	7.00	8.00	9.00

Note:- The first bus from Pontypridd is operated by the
Caerphilly U.D.C. and thereafter each alternate
bus is operated by the same Authority.

The first bus from Blackwood is operated by the
West Mon Omnibus Board, and thereafter each
alternate bus is operated by the same Authority.

The service Pontypridd to Treharris is operated
by the Pontypridd U.D.C.

1/6/46

In 1949 Roy Marshall caught former Wolverhampton Daimler COG5 No. 39 (JW 8113) at the terminus in Caerphilly. It carries bodywork by London-based coachbuilder Park Royal Coachworks Ltd.

between Ystrad Mynach and Markham. The route as extended was about 26 miles long and was in many ways a flagship for the two smaller participants: it was almost invariably operated by double-deckers and loadings were high, although the gradients were not as severe as on some services to the Valleys. Cardiff reparticipated from 9th September 1947 after their war time drawing back into the city.

Another new out of town service which began at this time, with effect from 28th March 1948, was from Caerphilly to Hendre, an area of Nantgarw, and Ty Rhiw, an estate above the settlement of Taff's Well, and this initially ran about six times a day, leaving the Caerphilly-Pontypridd service at Nantgarw and Cardiff-Tredegar service at Taff's Well. The manager soon complained that very little demand was being generated by it other than from school children.

On 27th March 1948 a short occasional service was commenced to the hospital annexe, then in use on Van Road to the east of the town, and on 27th June 1949 the Nelson service was diverted from its previous terminus near the old station to Bryncelyn, a new estate.

There were, however, some potential developments which never seemed to come to fruition. The proposition that the railway sell some extra land near the station had been ongoing since 1934. In 1948 British Railways, which had taken over from the GWR, finally agreed to sell the area, but the Council, which badly wanted the extra space, decided not to proceed at that stage, as the Ministry of Transport refused to loan them the relatively modest amount required. The issue continued thereafter to rumble slowly on.

On the other hand, there are always, even in the tedious minutiae of transport committee minutes, flashes of interest. In 1947 it was recorded that one of the drivers, E Eynon Evans, had left the Council's employment in order to become a full time writer. Emlyn Eynon Evans (1904-89) became a well known radio, television and film writer and appeared himself in a number of roles including parts in *I'm All Right Jack, Dixon of Dock Green,* and perhaps appropriately *Tiger Bay* – to which the Cardiff trolleybuses ran.

One of two double-deckers new in 1945 was this Guy Arab with Roe utility bodywork. Number 21 (FTG 121) was caught in 1952 pulling into the Station terminal.

The 1949 timetable showed services had developed so that they were as follows:

Caerphilly-Sengenydd;
Caerphilly-Ystrad Mynach-Nelson;
Cardiff-Nantgarw-Caerphilly-Ystrad Mynach-Blackwood-Markham-Tredegar (jointly with Cardiff Corporation and the West Monmouthshire Omnibus Board);
Caerphilly-Nantgarw-Pontypridd (jointly with Pontypridd UDC);
Caerphilly-Thornhill and Capel Gwilym;
Caerphilly-Nantgarw-Ty Rhiw;
Pontypridd-Treharris-Nelson-Ystrad Mynach-Blackwood (jointly with Pontypridd and Gelligaer UDCs and the West Monmouthshire Omnibus Board);
Caerphilly-Trecenydd and Penyrheol (town service);
Caerphilly-Miners' Hospital (town service);
Caerphilly-Van Road Hospital Annexe (town service).

The immediate post-War years also saw an influx of new vehicles, allowing these developing services to be run. The mileage run increased from 447,000 in 1940/1 to 886,000 in 1950/1. The years after 1945 saw a further consolidation of the place of double-deckers in the fleet, coupled with the introduction of some further single-deckers. In 1946 two more Guy Arabs were purchased, on this occasion with Strachans bodies. In company with other operators, Caerphilly continued to purchase Guys after the War after having being allocated them during the hostilities and having become accustomed to them. In 1948 four more Arabs arrived, this time with Willowbrook bodies, and in 1949 a further two, once again bodied by Strachans. They were used also on extras and workmen's services run to Senghenydd via St. Cenydd Road, but of course the main Aber Valley service continued single-deckered.

The post-War emphasis on double-deckers meant that fewer new single-deckers were required. However, four were ordered in 1947 from an unusual source. Fodens of Sandbach made a determined, but eventually unsuccessful, attempt to break into the public service vehicle market after the Second World War: prior to it they had constructed only experimental buses and had not attempted to sell widely. The new vehicle range was innovative in many respects, and in

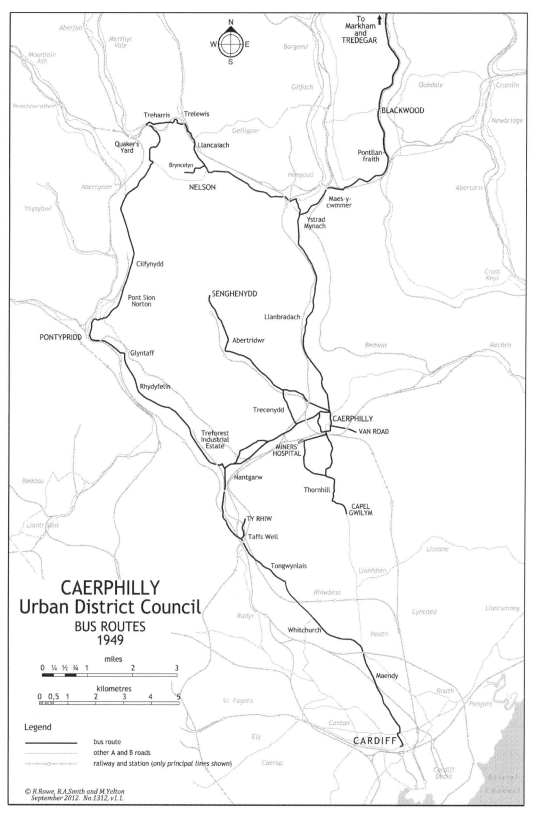

CAERPHILLY
Urban District Council
BUS ROUTES
1949

miles
0 ¼ ½ ¾ 1   2   3

kilometres
0 0,5 1   2   3   4   5

Legend
━━━━━ bus route
········· other A and B roads
╌╌╌╌╌ railway and station (only principal lines shown)

© R.Rowe, R.A.Smith and M.Yelton
September 2012. No.1312, v1.1.

For route details see page 67.

Strachan-bodied Guy Arab II No. 40 (FTG 240) is seen in 1952 about to leave on the joint service to Pontypridd.

By 1956 No. 41, the other Strachan-bodied Arab II, had been repainted with cream around the windows only, and with the circle around the fleet number no longer apparent. It waits departure on the short trip to Llanbradach.

times when new vehicles were at a premium Foden coaches sold well to independents. A small number of double-deckers was sold, some to nearby Merthyr. However, there was much less demand for their half-cab single-decker buses than for coaches.

Caerphilly had avoided involvement with local bodybuilders Welsh Metal Industries (WMI) after an argument over the cost of refurbishment work to one of the 1938 Dennis Lancets in 1946, which turned out to have been in a blessing in disguise: others who were attracted by WMI, such as neighbouring Bedwas, lived to regret their early enthusiasm. On 19th May 1948 WMI wrote formally to the Council, complaining that they were not getting any local support.

However, Caerphilly were attracted by the more professional approach taken by another Welsh based bodybuilder, Saunders of Beaumaris on Anglesey, who obtained a very substantial contract for the bodying of RT chassis for London Transport, and also other work around the country. They ordered two Foden PVSC5 chassis with Saunders bodies in February 1947 and then, after a visit to Anglesey, another two in September. Although there was a minor problem as early as 1948, which necessitated all four vehicles being returned to Saunders for repair, the Fodens went on to have reasonably long lives with the Council. Foden single-decker buses were relatively rare, but a high proportion of those which were constructed had Saunders bodies as the manufacturers sent 24 of the model to Beaumaris so that they would be available, as it were, off the peg. This was an attempt to cut through the delays in the supply of new vehicles at that time, and was the reason why Caerphilly were able to take delivery of the vehicles, including the additional two, so quickly.

In 1950 one of the more unusual of the many demonstrators used by Caerphilly arrived and was used for about a week on the Cardiff trunk route. This was KMA 575, a Foden double-decker with a Willowbrook body which was fitted with a two stroke engine manufactured by the constructors themselves. However, no orders for double-deckers went to Sandbach although Fodens tendered thereafter.

The demise of half-cab single-deckers and their replacement by underfloor-engined vehicles across the country was rapid and almost universal: it occurred in 1950 and 1951. In June 1950 a Leyland Olympic was on loan for demonstration: afterwards the manager said that he did not consider at that stage that the undertaking should acquire an underfloor-engined vehicle.

Following this recommendation, in 1951 an order was placed for another Foden single-decker, this time with bodywork by Bruce Coachbuilders of Cardiff, and also another three Guy Arab double-deckers, this time with Metro-Cammell bodies. None of the vehicles so ordered appeared.

The last front-engined single-decker ordered by Caerphilly was this Leyland PS2/5 (LTX 311), which is seen on trade plates prior to delivery at the Massey Bros factory in Pemberton, Wigan.

The single-deck order was moved to Leyland, and then when Bruce announced in November 1951 that they were to cease production as the immediate post-war demand had fallen away, the order was taken up by Massey Brothers of Pemberton, Wigan, which specialised in orders from the municipal market and which, as a relatively small operation itself, was able to accommodate short runs. It was to be the last half-cab single-decker to be taken by the Council, as unlike their neighbours, Gelligaer, who stayed loyal to front engined vehicles for some years thereafter, Caerphilly was soon to change its policy. The new arrival, LTX 311, was given the number 1 and arrived on 27th May 1952. It was on a relatively rare eight feet wide PS2/5 chassis: there is undoubtedly a reference in the minutes to it having been ordered as a PS2/7 coach chassis, but that may well have been simply an error, as it is difficult to see why the Council needed such a vehicle, although they had of course taken them second-hand during the War when there was no alternative. The result was an unusual vehicle which had a very full life with Caerphilly and in due course became the driver tuition and towing vehicle, surviving in that capacity until the end of the Council's own operations and later moving into preservation.

The order for Guy double-deckers was also abandoned, although it is not clear why, and in their lieu three Leyland PD2/12s with Leyland's own handsome bodies arrived. They introduced a revised livery scheme in which the cream bands were dispensed with and instead the window surrounds were painted cream. This was applied thereafter to double-deckers and, from the late 1950s, to single-deckers as well.

Six months after the arrival of that last half-cab, in December 1952, Caerphilly took delivery of two Leyland Royal Tigers, with Leyland's own angular bodywork, which introduced the underfloor-engined vehicle to the fleet. The minutes of the Omnibus Committee do not reveal why the manager had changed his mind, but, although there was no question at that stage of one-man-operation being reintroduced, the great advantage of the new type was the much increased capacity (44), which was particularly useful on the Senghenydd route. The practice had grown up by this time of the manager and the chairman travelling to the bodybuilders of each new batch to inspect the vehicles: a very careful eye was kept on cost, and when, for example, the issue of side destination blinds was raised and the committee were told that would be an extra £10 per vehicle, they declined to spend that amount.

On 15th April 1951 a new service to Energlyn Hospital via Court Road began, originally on an experimental basis. The new Penyrheol Estate was being developed not far from the terminus, and expansion was considered early on.

There were meetings at the end of that year with Merthyr with a view to connections being made between Caerphilly's Nelson (Bryncelyn) terminus and that of the other authority's route to Pentwyn Berthlwyd, which was very near, and although Caerphilly originally agreed to extend to meet Merthyr, in due course they asked Merthyr to extend to meet them. From 6th June 1952 Merthyr did indeed run through to make a connection, but a later census showed that very few people changed from one service to the other. There was even talk in late 1953 of a joint through service between the two towns, but nothing came of it.

In June 1952 it was decided to apply to run into the Penyrheol Estate from the Trecenydd side and an extension to Heol Tir Gibbon began: subsequently it was extended further into the estate, to Heol Fer. Later that year it was suggested that some Energlyn Hospital services be extended back to Bryn Glas, Penyrheol, but that was not done at that time. The service through Trecenydd developed steadily thereafter as the estates grew. As from 7th December 1953 a few journeys were run from Penyrheol direct to Abertridwr and Senghenydd, but they were little used and were abandoned with effect from 6th March 1954. In 1952 a joint service was started with West Mon from Blackwood via Caerphilly to Ninian Park, Cardiff, for Cardiff City and Wales football matches.

As from 29th March 1953 the main service to Senghenydd was increased in frequency from every 30 to every 20 minutes, against the advice of the manager, who thought extra traffic was best dealt with by duplicates.

The long-running issue of the BR land near to the station was then again raised and finally, 19 years after it was first proposed, on 24th February 1953 the Council agreed to buy the area in question for £650. It was developed over the next few years, with the fitting of some particularly unpleasant looking tall barriers to the side of the shelters, and rather ramshackle roofs above: it was not long

The third and fourth Fodens were acquired from Saunders Engineering (SEAS) stock in late 1947. In 1951 No. 12 (GTX 762) is seen in Blackwood.

Willowbrook-bodied Guy Arab II No. 42 of 1948, (HTX 442), is seen in 1966 in Station Terrace, after substantial rebuilding by the local authority, which included removal of the valences over the windows and of the side destination indicators. It is also in the revised livery style.

Blackwood High Street looks almost deserted as Willowbrook-bodied Guy No. 43 (HTX 443) passes on the long route from Tredegar to Cardiff in 1949.

Numbers 47 and 48, Strachan-bodied Guy Arab IIIs, were rebuilt about 1954 by a former employee of Bruce Coachworks and No. 48, (JTG 489), is shown in 1966, shortly before withdrawal, in Station Terrace. The constant parking of buses was a real interference with the peaceful enjoyment of the owners of the houses in the background.

Number 4 (LNY 904), a Leyland-bodied Titan PD2, was seen n Caerphilly about to leave for Nelson.

In 1969, shortly before conversion to a towing vehicle, No. 1 (LTX 311), by now in the more flattering new livery application, stands outside the older part of the garage in Mill Road. Note the Caerphilly Urban District Council lettering painted on the brickwork in abbreviated form above the office windows.

before it was said that more land was needed.

There was definitely an expansionist mood about the department at this time. It was even suggested that a second bus station be constructed at Twyn, in other words in the shopping centre just north of the Railway Station, but that was never taken forward. A more serious proposition was the need to rebuild and expand the garage and workshops either on the same site or elsewhere. Land at the eastern end of Bartlett Street, very near the terminus, was given consideration but the Ministry of Transport was unhappy about that.

However, there was less enthusiasm for out of the area running. Caerphilly wanted to cut back the Tredegar service to Blackwood, but at a meeting of the three joint operators on 17th February 1954 the others told them that it was undesirable and in particular that they could not unilaterally curtail their journeys. That came shortly after a proposition from Western Welsh that they, Caerphilly, and Pontypridd combine to run a through Pontypridd-Caerphilly-Newport service: that suggestion met with no enthusiasm at all from the Council.

Further route changes in the area took place in 1953/4 with a reorganisation of the former Jones Brothers services. There was further integration with Red & White, an unusual development for municipalities in the area, which largely ignored company operators. The Blackwood service was run direct from Pontypridd to Nelson, omitting Treharris and thus cutting out a low bridge, allowing for double-deck operation. The Pontypridd-Nelson-Bedlinog direct service was run entirely by Red & White, who numbered it 184, and a Pontypridd-Treharris-Nelson-Bedlinog service numbered 185 was run alternately by Red & White and the joint services. The Pontypridd-Treharris short journeys, also numbered 185, ran only on Saturdays and were run alternate weeks by Red & White and the municipalities. These changes came into effect on 7th February 1954.

In 1954 a further two Leyland Royal Tigers arrived: on this occasion, however, they carried Massey bodywork and they were in fact the first underfloor-engined chassis bodied by that firm, most of their work being with double-deckers. Another Leyland Titan also came that year, with Leyland body as with the previous three. Leyland appeared by this time to have become the Council's marque of choice. It is interesting

also that Longwell Green of Bristol, a small bodybuilder which obtained a great deal of work from the South Wales municipal operators, tendered for these bodywork contracts, but were not awarded orders for new vehicles then or later by Caerphilly, although they did do some refurbishment.

The route network was largely stable for the rest of the 1950s, but the labour supply began to be increasingly difficult. The pits were a more attractive occupation than they had been and there was an increase in light factory employment in the area. In July 1954 the revolutionary proposal was made to employ women as conductresses, which, unusually, was a step which had never been taken here, unlike other places, even in the War. The main problem was union opposition. It took until March 1956 before this was agreed, and a large number of women then came forward.

In 1956 Caerphilly went back to Leyland and took another Royal Tiger with Massey body: the chassis was new in 1951 and was reconditioned for sale by the manufacturers and fitted with its body. No doubt the financial saving for the purchaser was considerable.

The substantial expenditure required, however, was on the garage. A visit to Bournemouth was made to inspect that Corporation's state of the art premises and the same architects, Jackson & Greenen, were instructed. A very substantial reconstruction and extension, together with the provision of a new workshop, was carried out and was opened on 4th May 1959, at a cost of some £70,000. One consequence of this was that thereafter painting was carried out at various times for Bedwas, Gelligaer and West Mon and much of the heavy maintenance was also done for Bedwas.

In 1957, the undertaking continued with its now established preference for Leyland chassis and took two PD2/40 models. However, by this stage Leyland had ceased to construct their own bodywork and so, logically, the order went to Massey. It is noteworthy that the lowbridge body on these buses (which were fitted with staggered rather than bench-type seats upstairs) held only 55, or in other words only 11 more than the single-deckers which had been added to the fleet. In 1958 a further two vehicles of the same manufacture were acquired, but on this occasion their seating capacity was increased to 57.

The Council's conservative approach is well

Delivered in the same year as the last front-engined single-decker were two Leyland-bodied Royal Tigers, bought for use on the Senghenydd route where their extra capacity was required, as the photo shows. Number 6, (MNY 796), in the old application with little cream relief, pulls off in a cloud of smoke.

By 1969, shortly before withdrawal, No. 6 was relegated to the back route to Penyrheol. It is not clear whether No. 5 had ever had the trim at headlight level, but this vehicle certainly retained it to the end.

illustrated by their refusal on aesthetic grounds to allow external advertisements on their vehicles. They terminated all existing contracts with effect from 31st March 1958.

In 1960 it was decided that extra capacity was required for the double-deckers and two Leyland PD3/4s were purchased. It was unusual to see double-deckers built to the 30 feet length which had been introduced some years before being fitted with lowbridge bodywork, but Caerphilly had no other option available to them unless they had gone for one of the low-height double-deckers such as the Albion Lowlander or the Dennis Loline which were just coming on to the market. The Massey bodies on the Titans which arrived had 68 seats, a considerable advance on any other vehicles operated by the undertaking.

Rear-engined double-deckers, increasingly the mode form of transport in larger cities by this time, were not popular at all with the smaller South Wales municipalities, but later in 1960 Caerphilly did receive an Atlantean with Weymann lowbridge body on demonstration for two days. Orders did not follow at that time and in 1961 two more long Titans with Massey bodies arrived.

In common with other operators, although perhaps rather after them, since the ownership of cars locally was less than in some other places, use of the buses began to decline in the 1960s and economies were needed. As with other South Wales municipalities, one-man-operation was late in coming and resisted strongly before that time. There were relatively few changes to the route pattern, although there was particular pressure on the unremunerative former Jones operations, which so far as Caerphilly was concerned also required considerable dead mileage before taking up service. The Van Road service was withdrawn on 13th May 1956 as the hospital annexe had closed, but was then recommenced on 11th July 1956 when it reopened.

In 1960 the Penyrheol service via Court Road and Energlyn was approved but it was some time before it began because of the difficulty in arranging a turning point: eventually it was agreed to widen the corner of Heol Las and Penybryn. A works service began in late 1960 to Standard Box, Pentrebach, in Merthyr, but that did not last long. In 1962 a small bus station was opened in Ashgrove, Nelson, and the Caerphilly-Nelson (Bryncelyn) and Pontypridd-Blackwood services were diverted

into it. Shortly afterwards the Bryncelyn route was given a short circle at the terminus, returning to the bus station via Heol Mabon.

In late 1962 a somewhat unconventional vehicle for a municipality was purchased locally, in the shape of an Austin minibus with only eleven seats, which was not used on stage services. It often carried schoolchildren, including those from the hamlet of Groes wen, which had never been served by a regular service.

In early 1963 Caerphilly borrowed a Leyland Leopard with Willowbrook bus body from West Wales Motors of Tycroes in order to test clearances for a 36 ft bus. Again, there was a particular demand on the Senghenydd route, along which there was considerable population growth at the Caerphilly end. The trial was successful and shortly thereafter two Leopards arrived with Massey bus bodies, seating 55. However, the age of the double-decker was not yet over, and yet another PD3, also with Massey body, arrived, this time fitted with platform doors, which were of particular use on the long Cardiff-Tredegar service.

By early 1963 the long-established manager, Clifford Thomas, was ill and had to have long periods off. In the summer of 1963 he retired and was replaced by DAH O'Sullivan, who was to stay until the end of operations and then be appointed manager of the successor Rhymney Valley District Council undertaking. The Council thus had only three managers during its 54 years of running.

There was a poignant moment in the minutes in April 1963. A female passenger was killed by a Council bus at Treforest. It was solemnly agreed that the balance unused on her weekly ticket be refunded to her estate. The next year there was another: Western Welsh asked for permission to pick up local passengers on the 11.17 pm journey from Caerphilly to Ystrad Mynach, which would have provided a facility for the locals. They received a resounding no.

In 1964 two further Massey-bodied Leopards came to Caerphilly which were less boxlike than the earlier examples and were provided with wrap-round windscreens. In that year the Senghenydd branch line closed and for a number of years thereafter a subsidy was paid to the Council for extra services on the route. One very long running matter, the proposed extension of the Senghenydd service to Cenydd Terrace, which had resurfaced

The 1954 order for Leyland Royal Tigers had bodies by Massey Bros, Leyland by then having ceased building bus bodywork. In 1967 No. 7 (OTG 517) was still working, but was converted to one-man-operation. Here it returns to Caerphilly.

As mentioned in the text, Caerphilly pulled out of the ex-CMS pool in 1968. Shortly before they did so, No. 23 (YNY 923), a Massey-bodied Leyland PD2 of 1958, was seen in Blackwood, about to leave for Pontypridd.

After the earlier 30ft deliveries two further PD3s arrived in 1961. Number 29 (557 MNY) was at Penyrheol in 1966, displaying its classic Massey lines.

The first 36ft Leopards arrived in 1963 with Massey bodywork. In 1964, when still very new, No. 12 (12 SNY) demonstrates why double-deckers could not run along Mill Road.

Another two Massey-bodied 36ft Leopards arrived in 1964. Number 15 (ATX 515B) is seen in 1966 at the turning circle in Senghenydd, with the Terraces in the background which were never reached during the Council's operations.

The 1965 delivery of Leyland PD3s with Massey bodywork included platform doors. In 1969 No. 33 (GNY 433C) was captured on Station Terrace, showing its fine but undoubtedly dated lines, which were probably not appreciated by the houseowners since the vehicle was completely blocking the light from the cottages behind.

CAERPHILLY U.D. COUNCIL. TRANSPORT DEPARTMENT.

CAERPHILLY-NANTGARW-TREFOREST-PONTYPRIDD.   TGR. 272/6.

TIME TABLE.

WEEK DAYS.

		M.F.		M.F.					
	a.m.	a.m.	a.m.	a.m.	a.m.	a.m.	a.m.	and.	p.m.
Caerphilly	7.05	7.20	7.30	7.40	8.05	8.33	9.00	every	10.00
Industrial Estate	7.15	7.30	7.40	7.50	8.15	8.43	9.10	hour	10.10
Pontypridd	7.30	7.45	7.55	–	8.30	–	9.25	until	10.25

		M.F.		M.F.			
	a.m.	a.m.	a.m.	a.m.	a.m.	a.m.	a.m.
Pontypridd	6.25	6.45	6.55	7.10	7.35	8.30	–
Industrial Estate	6.35	6.55	7.05	7.20	7.45	8.40	8.44
Caerphilly	----	7.10	7.30	7.35	8.00	8.55	8.59

	a.m.	and	p.m.
Pontypridd	9.30	every	9.30
Industrial Estate	9.40	hour	9.40
Caerphilly	9.55	until	9.55

M.F. = Monday to Friday.

SUNDAYS.

	a.m.	p.m.	p.m.	p.m.	p.m.	p.m.	p.m.
Caerphilly	7.35	3.00	4.00	5.00	6.00	7.00	8.15
Industrial Estate	7.50	3.10	4.10	5.10	6.10	7.10	8.25
Pontypridd	---	3.25	4.25	5.25	6.25	7.25	8.40

	a.m.	p.m.	p.m.	p.m.	p.m.	p.m.	p.m.
Pontypridd	---	3.30	4.30	5.30	6.30	7.30	9.00
Industrial Estate	7.50	3.40	4.40	5.40	6.40	7.40	9.10
Caerphilly	8.00	3.53	4.55	5.55	6.55	7.55	9.25

Connections TO Senghenydd at Caerphilly Station.
Connections TO Llanbradach, Ystrad Mynach and Nelson at Castle Street,
Caerphilly.
Connections FROM Senghenydd at Castle St, Caerphilly.

November, 1962.

Timetables were a fairly rudimentary affair, produced on typewriters in the offices and then duplicated.

CAERPHILLY U.D. COUNCIL TRANSPORT: TGR.272/1
CARDIFF CORPORATION TRANSPORT.
WEST MON OMNIBUS BOARD.

CARDIFF/TREDEGAR JOINT SERVICE.

TIME TABLE.

MONDAYS TO FRIDAYS.

	a.m.	a.m.	a.m.	a.m.	a.m.	a.m.	a.m.		p.m.	p.m.	p.m.	p.m.
Cardiff	6.20					7.00	8.00		7.00	8.00	9.00	10.00
Nantgarw	6.45					7.19	8.28		7.28	8.28	9.28	10.28
Caerphilly	6.55				6.40	7.30	8.40	and	7.40	8.40	9.40	10.40
Llanbradach					6.50	7.40	8.50	every	7.50	8.50	9.50	10.50
Ystrad Mynach					7.00	7.45	9.00	hour	8.00	9.00	10.00	11.00
Pontllanfraith					7.05	7.55	9.05	until	8.05	9.05	10.05	11.05
Blackwood		6.10		6.15	7.15	8.15	9.15		8.15	9.15	10.15	11.10
Markham		6.23		6.28	7.28	8.28	9.28		8.28	9.28	10.28	
Tredegar				6.48	7.48	8.48	9.48		8.48	9.48	10.48	

	a.m.	a.m.	a.m.	a.m.	a.m.	a.m.	a.m.		p.m.	p.m.	p.m.	
Tredegar			*	7.12	8.12	9.12	10.12		9.12	10.12	10.50	
Markham		6.30	7.15	7.30	8.30	9.30	10.30		9.30	10.30	11.08	
Blackwood		6.40	7.25	7.40	8.40	9.40	10.40	and	9.40	10.40	11.23	
Pontllanfraith		6.45	7.30	7.45	8.45	9.45	10.45	every	9.45	10.45		
Ystrad Mynach		6.55	7.35	7.55	8.55	9.55	10.55	hour	9.55	10.55		
Llanbradach		7.05	7.40	8.05	9.05	10.05	11.05	until	10.05	11.05		
Caerphilly	6.55	7.14	7.50	8.14	9.14	10.14	11.14		10.14	11.14P		
Nantgarw	7.07	7.26	8.00	8.26	9.26	10.26	11.26		10.26			
Cardiff	7.33	7.52	8.25	8.52	9.52	10.52	11.52		10.52			

A Factory bus will leave Osband's Factory (Caerphilly) at 5.07p.m. each week night
for Blackwood and travel through to Cefn Fforest, Bedwellty & Markham (Work days only).

P = PICCADILLY.

FRIDAYS ONLY (Additional).

	p.m.	p.m.		p.m.	p.m.
Ystrad Mynach		2.30	and	8.30	9.30
Pontllanfraith		2.35	every	8.35	9.35
Blackwood		2.40	hour	8.40	9.40
Markham		2.53	until	8.53	
Markham		2.55	and	8.55	
Blackwood	2.10	3.10	every	9.10	
Pontllanfraith	2.15	3.15	hour	9.15	
Ystrad Mynach	2.25	3.25	until	9.25	

* Operates via Whitchurch By-Pass, last picking up
point Tongwynlais.

P.T.O.

3/64

CAERPHILLY U.D. COUNCIL. TRANSPORT DEPARTMENT.

S E N G H E N Y D D   R O U T E.   T I M E   T A B L E.   TGR.272/2.

WEEK DAYS (Mondays to Saturdays).

	a.m.	a.m.	a.m.	a.m.	a.m.		p.m.	p.m.	p.m.
Caerphilly	7.45	8.05	8.25	8.45	9.05	and	10.05	10.30	10.50
Penyrheol Sq.	7.48	8.13	8.33	8.53	9.13	every	10.13	10.38	10.58
Abertridwr	7.55	8.20	8.40	9.00	9.20	20	10.20	10.45	11.05
Senghenydd T.	8.05	8.30	8.50	9.10	9.30	mins	10.30	10.55	11.15
Senghenydd T.	8.05	8.35	8.55	9.15	9.35	and	10.35	10.55	11.15
Abertridwr	8.13	8.43	9.03	9.23	9.43	every	10.43	11.03	11.23
Penyrheol Sq.	8.20	8.50	9.10	9.30	9.50	20	---	---	---
Caerphilly	8.30	9.00	9.20	9.40	10.00	mins	G10.50	G11.10	G11.30

SUNDAYS.

	p.m.	p.m.	p.m.	p.m.	p.m.		p.m.	p.m.	p.m.
Caerphilly	12.10	1.30	2.25	2.45	3.05	and	10.05	10.30	10.40
Penyrheol Sq.	12.17	1.37	2.33	2.53	3.13	every	10.13	10.38	10.48
Abertridwr	12.25	1.41	2.40	3.00	3.20	20	10.20	10.45	10.55
Senghenydd T.	12.35	1.49	2.50	3.10	3.30	mins	10.30	10.55	11.05
Senghenydd T.	12.35	1.50	2.55	3.15	3.35	and	10.35	10.55	11.05
Abertridwr	12.40	1.57	3.00	3.23	3.43	every	10.43	11.03	11.13
Penyrheol Sq.	12.47	2.02	3.10	3.30	3.50	20	---	---	---
Caerphilly	12.55	H2.10	3.20	3.40	4.00	mins	G10.50	G11.10	G11.20

G = Garage. H = Hospital.

NOTE: Buses run direct from Senghenydd to Caerphilly Miners' Hospital
on - Saturdays at 1.35p.m.   Return from Hospital -
& 2.35p.m.   Saturdays at 3.02p.m.
Sundays at 1.50p.m.   Sundays at 3.40p.m.

Monday to Friday - a bus leaves the Miners' Hospital
for Caerphilly Station at 7.05p.m.

Buses run from Caerphilly (Station) to Van Road Hospital on Sundays
and Saturdays at 2.10p.m. They return from Van Road Hospital at
3.40p.m. on Sundays and 3.05p.m. on Saturdays.
Buses leave Van Road Hospital for Caerphilly Station at 7.05p.m.
Monday to Friday.

Connections at Caerphilly for Cardiff, Ystrad Mynach, Blackwood
and Tredegar.
Connections at Caerphilly (Castle St) for Pontypridd.
Connections at Piccadilly to and from Nelson, Llanbradach, etc.
Connections at Castle Street for Newport.

1st November, 1964.

regularly over the years, was partly dealt with by the construction of a new turning circle and an extension into an old quarry, with improvements to the footpath up to the Terraces.

In January 1965 a further attempt was made to curtail the trunk service from Cardiff at either Blackwood or Markham, and this was again rejected by the other partners: the West Mon Board was particularly anxious not to give up any running, and this was further demonstrated when the thorny issue of a through service from Caerphilly to Cardiff via Thornhill was raised yet again. The Board thought that such a service would adversely affect the existing tripartite service. Cardiff decided in 1965 to abandon their own service to Thornhill completely, but then finally, after about 30 years of stalling, agreed to joint running right through and this began in 1966.

In 1965 the need was for double-deckers again and three more 30ft Titans with Massey bodies and platform doors arrived. Despite the fact that in 1965 there was a further demonstration Atlantean in the town, the order for the following year was still conservative. In fact, in some ways it represented a throwback to earlier orders, since although two more Massey-bodied lowbridge Leyland Titans arrived and they were fitted with platform doors, they reverted to the shorter PD2 model, in this case of variant PD2/37, and seated only 60. They were of more use on the shorter services which penetrated housing estates, where the longer vehicles had difficulty with clearances. They were among the last lowbridge bodied buses supplied, although not as late as the well known 30ft example supplied to Bedwas & Machen in 1968.

In 1967 a further two double-deckers were supplied, but that was the final delivery for the Council of conventional front-engined vehicles. This pair, however, broke completely new ground, in that they were the first double-deckers in the fleet with front entrances and also with highbridge bodies, a change made possible only as a consequence of the demolition of some of the many low railway bridges in the area after the closure of the lines, particularly that at Maes-y-cwmmer on the Cardiff-Tredegar service: they seated 64. There is no indication of why the Committee was persuaded to change their long established practice as the manager's report is not filed.

Also in 1967 another Leopard with Massey body appeared, this time with a BET style front windscreen and dual-entrance layout and two more came the following year.

Caerphilly town was expanding fast by this time, and in January 1967 it was announced that a new service would be started to the Lansbury Park estate, one of the growing developments. This began on 13th March 1967, but was met on the first day by a human chain of residents of Castle Park, who objected to the route using Brynau Road.

By early 1968 the route pattern had evolved as follows, which was to remain largely unchanged until the end of the Council's operations in 1974:

Caerphilly-Senghenydd, every third journey running via Trecenydd;
Caerphilly-Ystrad Mynach-Nelson (Bryncelyn);
Cardiff-Nantgarw-Caerphilly-Ystrad Mynach-Blackwood-Markham-Tredegar (jointly with Cardiff Corporation and the West Monmouthshire Omnibus Board);
Caerphilly-Nantgarw-Pontypridd (jointly with Pontypridd UDC);
Caerphilly-Thornhill-Cardiff (jointly with Cardiff Corporation)
Glan-y-llyn-Ty Rhiw (Taff's Well local service);
Pontypridd-Nelson-Ystrad Mynach-Blackwood (jointly with Pontypridd and Gelligaer UDCs and the West Monmouthshire Omnibus Board);
Caerphilly-Penyrheol (direct and via Court Road) (town service);
Caerphilly-Lansbury Park (town service).

It will be seen that the through journeys to Ty Rhiw had ceased and been replaced by a short local service which connected it and another estate to the main road and station at Taff's Well. Hendre was no longer served.

As the 1960s went by, one-man-operation became the norm on many services elsewhere, but was strongly resisted here by the union. Passenger numbers on many routes fell off, albeit this was partially balanced in Caerphilly by population growth in some areas, which was an unusual development in the Valleys. In 1967 there was a damaging strike for several weeks, and experience showed that after not having access to buses many never returned to them. The formation of a joint board for the smaller municipalities of the Eastern Valleys recurred in different forms over the years:

The 1966 order reverted to the shorter Leyland PD2 model. Number 36 (LNY 536D), with Massey body, has since been preserved and restored. Here it turns off the main road towards Penyrheol in 1969.

In 1967 there was another new departure. The only single-decker bought that year, No. 51 (ONY 616F) was also a Leopard with Massey body, but had dual-entrances and a BET style front windscreen. It was photographed leaving town in 1968.

1967 also saw the arrival of two more PD2s, which were the first highbridge double-deckers in the fleet and the first with front entrances. Number 38, (ONY 638F), was leaving for Abertridwr on a sunny day in June 1969, with the doors still open.

Two Leopards with dual-entrance Massey bodies came in 1968. Number 17 (STX 217G) was later rebuilt to front entrance, but in 1969, while it still had both doors, it was caught near Abertridwr.

West Mon were implacably opposed to such a development, and what looked more feasible was a merger between Caerphilly and Bedwas, but one or other of the prospective participants always stood back.

The ex-CMS services posed particular difficulties and the dead mileage involved so far as Caerphilly were concerned made them even less economic than would otherwise have been the case. In June 1964 it was resolved that a two hourly, rather than hourly, service be operated on the Pontypridd-Blackwood service and that it be rediverted via Treharris, but this was not implemented. In June 1968, Caerphilly and Pontypridd gave notice to withdraw from the consortium which ran the routes, because the union would not agree to one-man-operation on them. They were thus left to Gelligaer, which had a strong interest in serving Bedlinog, and West Mon, which always hung on to any service into Blackwood, however inconvenient or unremunerative.

One-man-operation did finally commence in Caerphilly in the late 1960s, and in 1969 it was agreed to purchase two Leyland Panthers. However, the order must have been cancelled

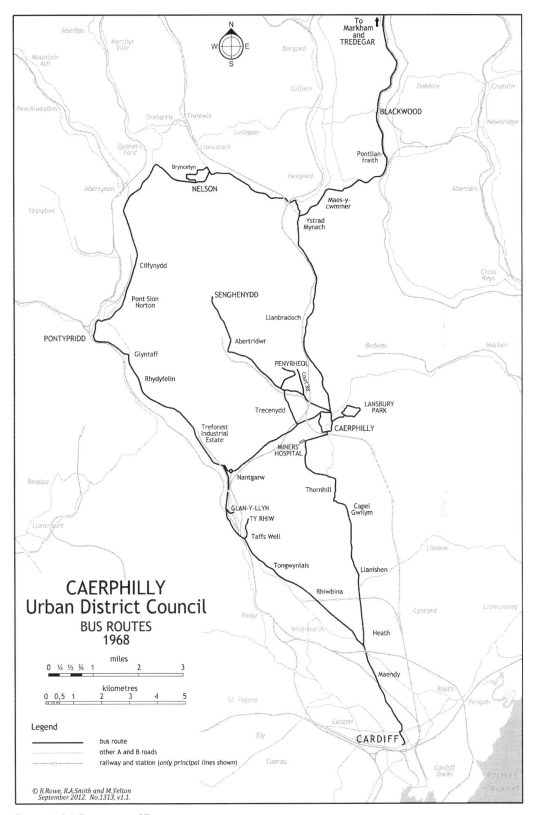

CAERPHILLY
Urban District Council
BUS ROUTES
1968

For route details see page 67.

In 1970 the two Leopards which were delivered had bodies by Northern Counties, which had taken over Massey. They were also shorter than the past few years' orders. Number 10 (WTG 610H) was running empty past the Cenotaph in the centre of Caerphilly when photographed in May 1972.

The second Leyland Leopard, No. 11 (WTG 611H), delivered in 1970, was seen when very new at Ystrad Mynach on the Caerphilly-Nelson service. The Northern Counties bodies had seats for 47 passengers and one front entrance/exit, unlike the previous Massey bodies.

Northern Counties also bodied the two Leopards which came in 1971, which reverted to longer chassis. Number 19 (BTX 419J) was leaving for Nelson in May 1972.

thereafter, no doubt to the benefit of the Council bearing in mind the troubles the model endured elsewhere, and in 1970 two shorter Leopards with Northern Counties B47F bodies arrived: Northern Counties, which also had considerable penetration into the municipal market, had by this time taken over their near neighbours Massey. These were the first two vehicles to be delivered ready equipped for one-man-operation and also pioneered a further livery variation which involved cream roofs, which were then applied throughout the fleet. The coat of arms of the Council was thereafter applied to the front upstairs side panels on double-deckers and towards the front on the side of single-deckers, instead of the previous practice of placing them centrally on the lower side panels. A fleet name of 'Caerphilly Council Transport' was applied. The resolution not to carry external advertisements however, continued.

In 1971 the coat of arms was modified after a competition among local school children, assisted by a prize of £10 from the Council, half of which was donated by the chairman of what was now termed the Transport Committee, and this too was applied to the vehicles as they were refurbished.

Also in 1971, two more Leopards arrived, but

they were constructed to the longer length which enabled the seating capacity to be increased to 53: a replacement minibus also came that year, but it was a Commer instead of an Austin.

In 1972 an almost unparalleled five new vehicles was taken into stock, as a determined attempt was made to eradicate older double-deckers and to extend the use of one-man-operation. These were all of the longer Leopard model, but had Willowbrook rather than Northern Counties bodies. By this stage the Council had effectively committed themselves to Leyland and did not invite competitive tenders.

The last vehicles purchased by Caerphilly UDC were in some ways among their more surprising additions. They purchased three Leyland Atlanteans of the advanced AN68 model, with East Lancs bodies and seating capacity for 78, much larger than anything else in the fleet. A further two were ordered for 1974 delivery, but in fact did not arrive until 1975, after the cessation of the undertaking: they went straight into the Rhymney Valley fleet. The decision to order the Atlanteans was made in late 1971, and again there is no indication of why the change of policy had been made, although it is noteworthy that earlier that year Gelligaer had

41

taken delivery of three Bristol VRs.

There was one further route development in the last years, which was the introduction of a new town service to Churchill Park via Mill Road. Perhaps more significantly, in 1973 the terminus area at Caerphilly was completely rebuilt and modernised, becoming much more attractive and user friendly. It has since been reconfigured yet again.

On 1st April 1974 Caerphilly Urban District disappeared into the new Rhymney Valley District in the new county of Mid-Glamorgan. The new authority also incorporated Gelligaer and Bedwas & Machen Urban Districts, both of which had of course operated buses, Rhymney Urban District, which had not, and part of Bedwellty Urban District, which with its neighbour Mynyddislwyn had set up the West Monmouthshire Omnibus Board. It was originally thought that the Board would continue in existence with Rhymney Valley as the minor participant and the new Islwyn Borough Council as the major. However, in the event the two new authorities fell out, the Board was dissolved, and Islwyn continued in existence on its own account.

The detailed history of the Rhymney Valley operation is outside the scope of this study, but in outline it initially adopted a conservative approach, simply continuing the existing operations although with a distinctive brown, cream and yellow livery. After deregulation it was reconstituted as Inter-Valley Link Ltd, using a similar livery but with more elaborate application and it expanded rapidly over a very wide area. However, as with most of the other South Wales municipal undertakings, the onset of deregulation destabilised the operations, and in due course it collapsed into the arms of National Welsh, which itself disappeared shortly thereafter. The Mill Road premises were cleared and the site was sold for retail purposes.

While most services in and around Caerphilly are now run by Stagecoach, it is a matter of no little irony that the next round of local government reorganisation in Wales reinvented Caerphilly, but on a much larger scale incorporating Islwyn, with its small post-West Mon operation. Thus Caerphilly once again became a transport operator, albeit in the changed conditions now prevailing in relation to such undertakings. That operation has now itself been sold.

The rebuilt bus station at Caerphilly opened in September 1973 and this shows it as new. Leopards of the Council board in the foreground: in the distance can be seen a Bristol Lodekka of Red & White and RE of Gelligaer on the through service from the Rhymney Valley to Newport, which had begun in 1968.

The arrival of the three 78-seat Atlanteans in 1973 finally gave the Council the capacity they had always craved for the Senghenydd route, provided they did not run via Mill Road. In April 1974, as Caerphilly operations ceased, No. 40 (NUH 40M) leaves for the Aber Valley via Trecenydd.

FLEET LIST

Fleet numbers were not allocated or carried until 1929 and so when set out below they refer only to the period after that.

Information is set out below as follows:

FLEET No.	REG'N NUMBER	CHASSIS	BODYWORK	SEATING

1920

1	KN 7902	Tilling-Stevens TS3	?	B32
2	KN 7903	Tilling-Stevens TS3	?	B32
3	TS 2569	Tilling-Stevens TS3	?	B32
4	TS 2679	Tilling-Stevens TS3	?	B32

These vehicles were both placed in service in 1920 to commence operations. 1 and 2 were registered by Tilling Stevens in Maidstone and were rebodied: 1 received a new body by W Lewis of Cardiff in 1927 and 2 by Aycliffe in 1926. The two other vehicles were ex-War Department and were registered in Dundee. They originally had lorry bodies, and were then given bus bodies in 1921 and these were again replaced in 1927 by Lewis. All four vehicles were withdrawn in about 1930.

1921

5	NY 371	Tilling-Stevens TS3	?	B26R
6	NY 372	Tilling-Stevens TS3	?	B26R
7	NY 373	Tilling-Stevens TS3	?	B26R

These three vehicles all had new fronts by W Lewis installed in 1927 and were withdrawn between about 1928 and 1932.

There are very few pictures of pre-1930 Caerphilly buses. This shows one of the 1921 Tilling-Stevens vehicles (NY 371-3), prior to registration. Low floors were not the order of the day.

1922

8	AX 1353	Dennis 40 Hp		Ch?

This vehicle was new in 1919 and was acquired from Ebbw Vale Steam Coal Company. It was given a new B26 body by J Norman of Cardiff in 1923 and in 1931 was withdrawn and fitted with a lorry body for use as a breakdown wagon.

1924

9	NY 5119	Tilling-Stevens TS3a	Norman	B28
10	NY 5540	Tilling-Stevens TS3a	Norman	B28

These two Tilling-Stevens had relatively short lives, being withdrawn in 1930. NY 5119 had a new front fitted by Caerphilly in 1928 after an accident.

1925

11	NY 9649	Tilling-Stevens TS3a	Norman	B30D

This vehicle was delivered with pneumatic tyres on the front wheels only: by late 1931 it was being used only as a breakdown vehicle.

1928

12	TX 5779	Tilling-Stevens B10A2	W Lewis	B32D
12A	TX 5894	Tilling-Stevens B10A2	W Lewis	B32D
14	TX 5993	Vulcan Blackpool	W Lewis	B19F
15	TX 6050	Tilling-Stevens B10A2	W Lewis	B32D
16	TX 6094	Vulcan Blackpool	W Lewis	B19F
17	TX 6358	Tilling-Stevens B10A2	W Lewis	B32D
18	TX 6380	Tilling-Stevens B10A2	W Lewis	B32D

In 1927 the Council had demonstrations by both Tilling-Stevens and Thornycroft and decided to stay with the former manufacturer. They would not use number 13: hence the use of 12A. The two Vulcans were used as one-man buses, initially on the Nelson route and later on Pontypridd. All this year's entry of vehicles were withdrawn between 1936 and 1939. The bodybuilder, Lewis, was a Tilling-Stevens agent in Cardiff.

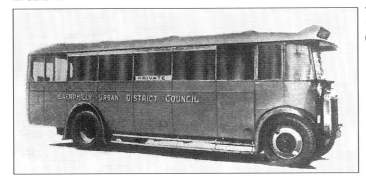

This shows the offside of one of the 1928 Tilling-Stevens: No. 18 (TX 6380) in the original red livery.

1930

19	TX 9238	Tilling-Stevens B10A2	Eastwood & Kenning	B32D
20	TX 9240	Tilling-Stevens B10A2	Eastwood & Kenning	B32D
21	TX 9242	Tilling-Stevens B10A2	Eastwood & Kenning	B32D
22	TX 9244	Tilling-Stevens B10A2	Eastwood & Kenning	B32D
	DK 3443	Guy B	Strachan & Brown	B26F
	DK 3444	Guy B	Strachan & Brown	B26F
	?	Guy	?	B30
	?	Guy	?	B30

A further batch of Tilling-Stevens vehicles was delivered in 1930: the bodies were intended originally to be by Davidson but this was changed to Eastwood & Kenning. 19, 21 and 22 were withdrawn in 1939 but

20 stayed in service until 1944, when it was burned out in the depot fire of that year. The four second-hand Guys, were used only until 1933 and details of two of them are very scant. The first two were originally owned by Rochdale Corporation, and the fourth had been reconstructed by Guys in Wolverhampton.

1933

23	TG 5853	Thornycroft CD 6LW	Beadle	B32R
24	TG 5854	Thornycroft CD 6LW	Beadle	B32R
25	TG 6531	Thornycroft CD 6LW	Beadle	B32R

In 1933 the Council's allegiance to Tilling-Stevens was broken because that supplier could not provide vehicles with Gardner 6LW engines, so the order was given to Thornycroft, which had angled hard for business over the preceding years. The third vehicle, 25, was exhibited on the Beadle stand at the Commercial Vehicle Show at Olympia in November 1933 in Caerphilly livery, and was then bought by the undertaking. These three vehicles lasted throughout the war years and were withdrawn in 1948/9.

Commercial Motor for 1934 showed No. 23 (TG 5853), one of the 1933 delivery of Thornycrofts with Beadle rear entrance bodywork.

1936

26	ATG 136	Dennis Lancet	Dennis	B32R
27	ATG 235	Dennis Lancet	Dennis	B32R
28	ATG 632	Dennis Ace	Dennis	FB20F
29	ATG 633	Dennis Ace	Dennis	FB20F

A frontal view of Dennis Lancet No. 26 (ATG 136) in somewhat rundown condition in the garage yard, possibly while being used as a recovery vehicle in the early 1950s.

Facing Page: An offside view of No.31 (CTX 947), taken in 1952 after further rebuilding by the Council.

In 1936 Caerphilly entered upon its Dennis phase. The two Lancets were not entirely satisfactory buys, as in 1937 they both had their Dennis Lanova engines replaced by Dennis 04 units, and in 1939 their bodies required complete rebuilding. 26 was reconditioned by Romilly Motors in Cardiff in 1946: it had been suggested that Burlingham should rebody both of them in 1944, but that was not done. 26 was used as a towing vehicle between 1951 and 1955 and 27 was withdrawn in 1948. The two forward control Dennis Aces were used as one-man vehicles but then had their capacity increased to 26 in 1941. No. 29 was destroyed in the depot fire but 28 lasted until 1948.

1937

30	CTG 303	Dennis Ace	Dennis	FB20F

This was also used as a one-man vehicle, initially on the Trecenydd route: it was withdrawn in 1947.

In 1937 *Commercial Motor* featured the third Dennis Ace supplied as a one-man vehicle to Caerphilly, No. 30 (CTG 303), which was largely used on the short run to Trecenydd.

1938

31	CTX 947	Dennis Lancet II	Dennis	B32R
32	CTX 948	Dennis Lancet II	Dennis	B32R
33	DTX 48	Daimler COG5/40	Willowbrook	B39R

The first Daimler in the fleet was Willowbrook show model No. 33 (DTX 48), seen about to leave Caerphilly for Senghenydd in 1949.

These two Dennis Lancets were supplied with Dennis 04 engines, which were replaced in 1939: the bodies were repaired in 1938. 32 was destroyed in the depot fire of 1944, but 31 was rebuilt locally by Welsh Metal Industries in 1946: the resulting arguments meant that the firm was never again employed by the Council. It was again rebuilt in the operator's own workshops in 1951 and lasted until 1953. 33 was the first Daimler in the fleet and was a show model prepared by the bodybuilders. It was withdrawn in 1954.

1939

34	DTX 836	Daimler COG5/40	Willowbrook	B38R
35	ETG 647	Daimler COG5/40	Willowbrook	B35R
36	ETG 680	Daimler COG5/40	Willowbrook	B35R

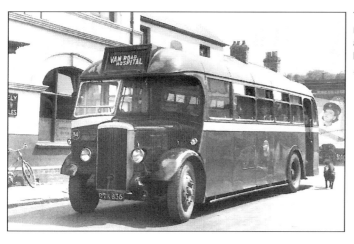

The second Daimler to arrive had a rear entrance body by Willowbrook and is dressed for a short run to Van Road from Caerphilly in July 1949.

Following the experience with the 1938 Daimler, three more arrived the following year. 36 was lost in the 1944 fire, but the remaining two ran until 1954, both having undergone some rebuilding.

1941

| 7 | TH 5507 | Albion SPPV70 | Plaxton | C35F |

The Council's need for further vehicles during a period when new buses were in very short supply was such that they purchased this 1935 petrol-engined Albion second-hand from HG Sage and Son of Burry Port, West Wales. It was damaged in accidents in 1942 and again in 1944, and then rebuilt in 1949 before being withdrawn the following year.

The desperation of the Council to obtain vehicles during the War resulted in the acquisition of this petrol-engined Albion from Sage of Burry Port, which was rebuilt in 1949 and is shown in 1950, the year it was withdrawn.

1942

9	ETX 649	Albion CX13	Duple	B35F
6	VD 1536	Daimler CP6	Pickering	B32R

The last Albion built before the cessation of production of passenger vehicles for the duration of the War was ordered by Red & White with a centre entrance, but was diverted to Caerphilly and altered to a more conventional front entrance. It stayed until 1954. The Daimler was another short term expedient and its time with the UDC was short as it was destroyed by fire in 1944. It had been new to Lanarkshire Traction in 1932, but was acquired from GF Rees of Neyland, who acquired it just before the War.

1943

14	FNY 414	Daimler CWA6	Duple	L27/28R
8	FNY 308	Albion CX13	Plaxton	FC32F
21	WN 9571	Tilling-Stevens HA39A7	Park Royal	C32F

On Roy Marshall's productive visit in 1949 he caught Daimler No. 14 (FNY 414) the first double-decker in the fleet at the rear of the garage. The utility body by Duple was later comprehensively rebuilt.

The first double-decker run by Caerphilly arrived in August 1943, although the previous year had seen the loan for a few days of a Guy Arab from Pontypridd, presumably for driver training. It was dismantled in 1951 and completely rebuilt over the next three years, re-entering service in 1954 and being withdrawn in 1960. The Albion was new in 1939 as BTH 20 with a petrol engine, and again ran for Sage of Burry Port before being acquired and reregistered by the RAF. It was the vehicle in which the fire started and it was lost in the conflagration. The Tilling-Stevens was another second-hand addition: it was new to Bullens of Swansea in 1936 and ran for Caerphilly for only about 8 months before being burned out with the Albion.

1944

15	FNY 515	Daimler CWA6	Duple	L27/28R
16	FNY 716	Daimler CWA6	Duple	L27/28R
17	FNY 717	Daimler CWA6	Duple	L27/28R
18	FNY 718	Guy Arab II 6LW	Roe	L27/28R
19	FNY 719	Guy Arab II 6LW	Roe	L27/28R
4	JW 5794	Guy Arab 5LW	Park Royal	B32R
5	JW 5795	Guy Arab 5LW	Park Royal	B32R
39	JW 8113	Daimler COG5	Park Royal	B34R
37	JW 8117	Daimler COG5	Park Royal	B34R
38	JW 8118	Daimler COG5	Park Royal	B34R

The two Daimler utilities which arrived just after the 1944 fire, Nos. 16 and 17 (FNY 716/7), sit next to each other in the yard in 1952. They both had Duple bodies which were rebuilt in 1950 by Longwell Green, a bodybuilder which never supplied any complete vehicles to Caerphilly.

1944 saw the arrival of an unprecedented number of vehicles as the Council sought to struggle with the strains resulting from the War and the conveyance of workers to factories and pits. The situation was made far worse in Caerphilly by the fire at the depot in April 1944 which resulted in the destruction of eight vehicles, about one third of the fleet, and the necessity to obtain second-hand replacements quickly. The first of the utility Daimlers, 15, was in service for only a few weeks before being severely damaged by the conflagration: it was sent for repair but then the chassis was sold to Swan Motor Company of Swansea and a new Northern Coachbuilders highbridge body was fitted: it later passed to United Welsh. The other

Daimlers, 16 and 17, arrived just after the fire. No.17 was repaired after accident damage the next year and they were both rebuilt by Longwell Green in 1950, lasting then until 1957. The Guys lasted longer: 18 was rebuilt by the Council in about 1956 and then in 1961 became a driver training vehicle and in 1968 a breakdown truck: 19 was withdrawn in 1963. The five single-deckers were acquired in late 1944 from Wolverhampton Corporation, which had used them on their extensive network of country services, for which they were fitted with roof racks: the Guys dated from 1934 and the Daimlers from 1936. 37-9 operated for a time in their former livery. Most of these vehicles were withdrawn in 1951, but 37 and 39 lasted until 1953.

Roe-bodied Guy utility No. 18 (FNY 718) is seen at the garage. The date is not recorded but it was clearly after repainting in the new application of the livery and after rebuilding by the Council in 1956.

Looking somewhat run-down and with a loose side to the bonnet, former Wolverhampton Corporation Guy No. 5 (JW 5795) waits by the Railway Hotel in Caerphilly in 1949.

A busy scene at the terminus in 1956 with 20 (FNY 820), the Weymann-bodied Guy which had been delivered in 1945.

One of the vehicles taken into stock by Caerphilly on the joint acquisition of Jones Brothers of Treharris was No. 32 (HB 5455), a Willowbrook-bodied Dennis Lancet, which is seen in 1949 on the then new service to Ty Rhiw via Taff's Well.

1945

20	FNY 820	Guy Arab II	Weymann	L27/28R
21	FTG 121	Guy Arab II	Roe	L27/28R
32	HB 5455	Dennis Lancet II	Willowbrook	B35F
1	HB 5986	Bedford OWB	Duple	B32F

Two more Arabs arrived in 1945, both of which were later rebuilt but stayed until 1959 and 1965 respectively, and then as its share of the running stock of Jones Brothers, Caerphilly received three vehicles. WO 6573, a 1932 Dennis Lancet with Weymann B31R body, was never used or numbered. The other Lancet was new in 1938 and fitted in with the fleet: it lasted in service until 1954 and was then used as a towing truck until 1959. The Bedford OWB was sold in 1948: its capacity was too small for most of the work at that time.

1946

40	FTG 240	Guy Arab II 6LW	Strachans	L27/28R
41	FTG 241	Guy Arab II 6LW	Strachans	L27/28R

The two further Guy Arabs were later rebuilt by the Council and 41 was further rebuilt in 1955 after accident damage. Both lasted until 1965 and were then exported to Africa.

One of the 1946 Arabs, No. 41 (FTG 241), is seen in the old livery application in 1954 with the helpful but common destination 'Relief'.

The first Foden in the fleet, No. 10 (GTX 310) was captured on film in 1949, when only two years old, ready to leave on the busy route to Senghenydd.

1947

10	GTX 310	Foden PVSC5	Saunders	B36F
11	GTX 311	Foden PVSC5	Saunders	B36F
12	GTX 762	Foden PVSC5	Saunders	B35F
13	GTX 763	Foden PVSC5	Saunders	B35F

In 1947, when new vehicles were still in short supply, two Fodens were ordered with Welsh-built bodywork by Saunders of Beaumaris. After a visit there in September 1947, a further two were ordered, as they were available at short notice and indeed arrived by December that year. 10 and 11 were rebuilt by the Council in 1956 and lasted until 1963: 12 and 13 went in 1959.

1948

42	HTX 442	Guy Arab II 6LW	Willowbrook	L27/26R
43	HTX 443	Guy Arab II 6LW	Willowbrook	L27/26R
44	HTX 444	Guy Arab II 6LW	Willowbrook	L27/26R
45	HTX 445	Guy Arab II 6LW	Willowbrook	L27/26R

Willowbrook-bodied Guy Arab No. 42 (HTX 442) arrived in 1948 and is seen in as delivered condition in July 1949 at the garage.

Strachan-bodied Guy No. 47 (JTG 478) is seen in 1951 heading south along a deserted Blackwood High Street towards Caerphilly and Cardiff.

As with many other operators, Caerphilly continued to order Guys after having them imposed upon them during the War. All these vehicles lasted a substantial time in the fleet, being withdrawn between 1966 and 1968, but all had been subject to some rebuilding by the Council, including removing the window valences and the side indicators over the rear platform.

1949

| 47 | JTG 478 | Guy Arab III 6LW | Strachans | L27/26R |
| 48 | JTG 489 | Guy Arab III 6LW | Strachans | L27/26R |

These Guys were completely rebuilt by Caerphilly themselves in about 1954 and so lasted until 1965/6. The work was carried out by an employee who had previously worked for Bruce Coachworks in Cardiff.

1951

2	LNY 902	Leyland PD2/12	Leyland	L27/28R
3	LNY 903	Leyland PD2/12	Leyland	L27/28R
4	LNY 904	Leyland PD2/12	Leyland	L27/28R

The arrival of Leyland double-eckers in 1951 ushered in an era in which all new vehicles were of that marque. Number 4 (LNY 904) is seen in Pontypridd on the ex-CMS service to Blackwood in 1956.

The last half-cab single-decker to be delivered, No. 1 (LTX 311), is seen in 1952, shortly after arriving, in the old livery application, and has loaded for Senghenydd.

Although an order for three further Guys was placed, in due course this was moved to Leyland and three robust Titans of classic design arrived. They lasted until 1968/9 (2/3) or 1971 (4), which spent its last few months on loan to Gelligaer.

1952

1	LTX 311	Leyland PS2/5	Massey	B35F
5	MNY 795	Leyland PSU1/13	Leyland	B44F
6	MNY 796	Leyland PSU1/13	Leyland	B44F

The Leyland half -cab single-decker which arrived in 1952 was a late model and was 8 feet wide: it was intended to have Bruce bodywork but on the closure of that firm the order was taken on by Massey. It was withdrawn in 1969 and became a learner and towing vehicle, passing as such to RVDC. The other two vehicles were the first underfloor-engined single-deckers in the fleet and after rebuilding by the Council in 1961 lasted until 1970/1.

By 1969, shortly before withdrawal, No. 5 (MNY 795), was in Caerphilly, without headlight trim.

The first bodies constructed by Massey on underfloor-engined vehicles were Caerphilly's Royal Tigers Nos. 7 and 8. Here 7 (OTG 517) displays its offside cab door before leaving for the Aber Valley in 1956.

1954

7	OTG 517	Leyland PSU1/13	Massey	B44F
8	OTG 518	Leyland PSU1/13	Massey	B44F
26	OTG 526	Leyland PD2/12	Leyland	L27/28R

The only double-decker supplied in 1954 was No. 26 (OTG 526), the last to be bodied for the Council by Leyland. Here it is seen at Penyrheol about to run back into town, in 1968.

The orders for 1954 replicated those of earlier years, save that the Royal Tigers had Massey bodies, the first to be manufactured by that company on an underfloor-engined chassis. They were converted for one-man-operation in 1967. All three vehicles were withdrawn in 1972.

1956

9	UTX 9	Leyland PSU1/13	Massey	B44F

The chassis of this vehicle dated from 1951: it was reconditioned by Leyland, fitted with a new Massey body and lasted until 1972.

No new vehicles were delivered in 1955 and only one in 1956, and that was a reconditioned chassis from 1951 fitted with a new Massey body. No. 9 (UTX 9) was still two manned in 1968.

24	VTX 24	Leyland PD2/40	Massey	L27/28R
25	VTX 25	Leyland PD2/40	Massey	L27/28R

The two Leylands supplied in 1957 had the first Massey double-deck bodies supplied to the undertaking. They were fitted from new with heaters and had staggered rather than straight seating on the upper deck. They lasted until 1972/3.

The first Massey double-deck bodies for Caerphilly came in the form of two Leyland PD2/40s with staggered seating upstairs, which arrived in 1957. Number 24 (VTX 24) was outside the garage in 1969.

In 1958 two further PD2s with Massey lowbridge bodies appeared. Number 22 (YNY 922) was in the Station area in 1966.

1958

22	YNY 922	Leyland PD2/40	Massey	L29/28R
23	YNY 923	Leyland PD2/40	Massey	L29/28R

These were similar to those supplied the previous year, save for the slightly increased capacity. 22 was lent to and then in 1971 sold to Gelligaer: 23 passed to RVDC.

1960

27	827 HNY	Leyland PD3/4	Massey	L35/33R
28	828 HNY	Leyland PD3/4	Massey	L35/33R

The first two 30ft long double-deckers reflected the increased need for larger vehicles. They were of traditional design, with lowbridge bodies and exposed radiators and were fitted with rear facing bulkhead seats. They were withdrawn shortly before the end of operations in 1974.

1960 saw the arrival of the first 30ft double-deckers. In 1966 No. 27 (827 HNY) was about to leave on the short run to the Hospital, for which its capacity of 68 was unlikely to be tested.

Also in 1966, but in Caerphilly, was No. 30 (558 MNY) seen from the nearside, standing by the Railway Hotel.

1961

29	557 MNY	Leyland PD3/4	Massey	L35/33R
30	558 MNY	Leyland PD3/4	Massey	L35/33R

These vehicles were similar to those supplied the previous year, but were transferred to RVDC in 1974.

1963

12	12 SNY	Leyland PSU3/1R	Massey	B55F
13	13 SNY	Leyland PSU3/1R	Massey	B55F
31	31 SNY	Leyland PD3/4	Massey	L35/33RD
49	895 UTG	Austin J02BA	Austin	11

The first 36ft single-deckers, Nos. 12 and 13 (12/3 SNY), came in 1963 and were largely used on the route to Senghenydd, from which 13 was returning in 1966.

An unusual vehicle for a municipal operator was No. 49 (895 UTG), an Austin minibus bought for school services in 1963, seen outside the garage.

The solitary double-decker which came in 1963 was No. 31 (31 SNY), the first with platform doors, seen in 1967 about to leave on the short trip to Llanbradach.

The first 36ft long vehicles in the fleet, especially useful for the Senghenydd service, were 12 and 13. In that year another PD3 arrived, this time with platform doors: all of these three passed to RVDC. The remaining vehicle delivered in 1963 was a minibus (as also used by West Mon and Gelligaer), which was sold in 1972.

1964

14	ATX 514B	Leyland PSU3/1R	Massey	B55F
15	ATX 515B	Leyland PSU3/1R	Massey	B55F

A further two Massey-bodied single-deckers arrived in 1964, but they had wrap round windscreens. Number 14 was painted in a special livery for the investiture of the Prince of Wales in 1969, as was also done to a Gelligaer bus. All passed to RVDC.

In 1964 the Council took delivery of two long Leyland Leopards with Massey bodies. In 1969 No. 14 (ATX 514B) was given a special livery for the investiture of the Prince of Wales and is seen that year in Abertridwr.

1965

32	GNY 432C	Leyland PD3/4	Massey	L35/33RD
33	GNY 433C	Leyland PD3/4	Massey	L35/33RD
34	GTX 734C	Leyland PD3/4	Massey	L35/33RD

Three similar PD3s came in 1965 and all survived to run for RVDC.

In 1965 three further PD3s with Massey bodies and platform doors arrived. In 1966 No. 32 (GNY 432C) was seen at Penyrheol

1966

35	LNY 535D	Leyland PD2/37	Massey	L31/29RD
36	LNY 536D	Leyland PD2/37	Massey	L31/29RD

1966 saw a reversion to shorter Titans with staggered seating upstairs. 36 has since been preserved and restored to its Caerphilly livery.

One of the pair of 1966 Leyland Titans, yet again with platform doors. 35 (LNY 535D) was seen in 1967 in Cardiff bus station.

1967

16	ONY 616F	Leyland PSU3/1R	Massey	B51D
37	ONY 637F	Leyland PD2/37	Massey	H37/27F
38	ONY 638F	Leyland PD2/37	Massey	H37/27F

1967 saw another three Leylands with Massey bodies. The single-decker had a BET style front windscreen: the double-deckers were the first highbridges in the fleet and also introduced front entrances. All went to RVDC.

Number 16 (ONY 616F) returns to Caerphilly when still very new, in early 1968.

When still new, No. 37 (ONY 637F) is seen at an unknown location en route for Caerphilly.

1968

17	STX 217G	Leyland PSU3A/2R	Massey	B51D
18	STX 218G	Leyland PSU3A/2R	Massey	B51D

These were two further Leyland Leopards with Massey bodies: in 1974 17 was rebuilt to B51F and fitted for one-man-operation. Both passed to RVDC.

The second 1968 Leopard, No.18 (STX 218G), was never rebuilt. In early 1969, with snow on the ground, it makes for Senghenydd displaying both doors.

1970

10	WTG 610H	Leyland PSU4A/2R	Northern Counties	B47F
11	WTG 611H	Leyland PSU4A/2R	Northern Counties	B47F

The next two Leopards acquired had to have a new bodybuilder, as Massey had been taken over by Northern Counties. These vehicles were of shorter length and had wrap round windscreens. They passed to RVDC.

A small girl on the entrance step queries the camera as No.10 (WTG 610H) waits at the Railway Hotel to leave for Penyrheol in May 1972.

1971

19	BTX 419J	Leyland PSU3B2R	Northern Counties	B53F
20	BTX 420J	Leyland PSU3B/2R	Northern Counties	B53F
48	ETG 48K	Commer 2500LB	Rootes	12

Two of the longer Leopards bodied by Northern Counties arrived in 1971, together with a minibus, all of which passed to RVDC.

A close up view of the offside of No. 19 (BTX 419J), after arriving at the terminus.

The replacement for the Austin minibus was a Commer, No. 48 (ETG 48K), which came in 1971 and was seen in 1973 at the garage.

1972

1	ETG 111K	Leyland PSU3B/2R	Willowbrook	B53F
2	ETG 112K	Leyland PSU3B/2R	Willowbrook	B53F
3	ETG 113K	Leyland PSU3B/2R	Willowbrook	B53F
4	KNY 924L	Leyland PSU3B/2R	Willowbrook	B53F
5	KNY 925L	Leyland PSU3B/2R	Willowbrook	B53F

1972 saw a change of bodybuilder to Willowbrook, which supplied five of the longer Leopards: a similar vehicle was supplied in that year to Bedwas & Machen. All passed to RVDC.

There was a return to Willowbrook in 1972 when five longer Leopards arrived. A well loaded No. 2 (ETG 112K) is leaving for Trecenydd and Penyrheol in 1973.

1973

39	NUH 39M	Leyland AN68/1R	East Lancs	H45/33F
40	NUH 40M	Leyland AN68/1R	East Lancs	H45/33F
41	NUH 41M	Leyland AN68/1R	East Lancs	H45/33F

The final delivery of vehicles to the undertaking was a real departure from tradition and a further two Atlanteans were on order for 1974.

The arrival of the three 78 seat Atlanteans in 1973 finally gave the Council the capacity they had always craved for the Senghenydd route, provided they did not run via Mill Road. In 1974, as Caerphilly operations ceased, No. 40 (NUH 40M) is returning to Caerphilly almost empty from Senghenydd.

Caerphilly bus routes shown on the maps

Page 9

Ystrad Mynach-Nelson;

Cardiff-Nantgarw-Caerphilly-Ystrad Mynach-Blackwood-Markham (jointly with Cardiff Corporation and the West Monmouthshire Omnibus Board);

Caerphilly-Senghenydd;

Caerphilly-Trecenydd (town service), Fridays and Saturdays only.

Page 20

The 1949 timetable showed services had developed so that they were as follows:

Caerphilly-Senghenydd;

Caerphilly-Ystrad Mynach-Nelson;

Cardiff-Nantgarw-Caerphilly-Ystrad Mynach-Blackwood-Markham-Tredegar (jointly with Cardiff Corporation and the West Monmouthshire Omnibus Board);

Caerphilly-Nantgarw-Pontypridd (jointly with Pontypridd UDC);

Caerphilly-Thornhill and Capel Gwilym;

Caerphilly-Nantgarw-Ty Rhiw;

Pontypridd-Treharris-Nelson-Ystrad Mynach-Blackwood (jointly with Pontypridd and Gelligaer UDCs and the West Monmouthshire Omnibus Board);

Caerphilly-Trecenydd and Penyrheol (town service);

Caerphilly-Miners' Hospital (town service);

Caerphilly-Van Road Hospital Annexe (town service).

Page 39

By early 1968 the route pattern had evolved as follows, which was to remain largely unchanged until the end of the Council's operations in 1974:

Caerphilly-Senghenydd, every third journey running via Trecenydd;

Caerphilly-Ystrad Mynach-Nelson (Bryncelyn);

Cardiff-Nantgarw-Caerphilly-Ystrad Mynach-Blackwood-Markham-Tredegar (jointly with Cardiff Corporation and the West Monmouthshire Omnibus Board);

Caerphilly-Nantgarw-Pontypridd (jointly with Pontypridd UDC);

Caerphilly-Thornhill-Cardiff (jointly with Cardiff Corporation)

Glan-y-llyn-Ty Rhiw (Taff's Well local service);

Pontypridd-Nelson-Ystrad Mynach-Blackwood (jointly with Pontypridd and Gelligaer UDCs and the West Monmouthshire Omnibus Board);

Caerphilly-Penyrheol (direct and via Court Road) (town service);

Caerphilly-Lansbury Park (town service).V

A fine example of a preserved Caerphilly vehicle is this Leyland Titan PD2, with its traditional and instantly recognisable Massey lowbridge bodywork. It was seen at a rally in Cumbria and the neat arrangement of the rear platform doors will be noted. Number 36,(LNY 536D) was delivered in 1966. (John A Senior)

Acknowledgements

All of the black and white photographs in the book are from the camera or collection of Roy Marshall to whom we record our thanks. We are grateful to David and Mary Shaw for their meticulous proof-reading of the text.

Michael Yelton
November 2012